A Vow Fulfilled
The Fran Laufer Story:
Memories and Miracles

Fran Laufer

A TARGUM PRESS BOOK

First published 2009
Copyright © 2009 by Fran Laufer
ISBN 978-1-56871-502-5

Published and distributed by:
TARGUM PRESS, INC.
22700 W. Eleven Mile Rd.
Southfield, MI 48034
E-mail: targum@targum.com
Fax: 888-298-9992
www.targum.com

Distributed by:
FELDHEIM PUBLISHERS
208 Airport Executive Park
Nanuet, NY 10954

Printed in Israel by Chish

Yeshiva University
Center for the Jewish Future

Fran Laufer's life is a testament to the tenacity of the human spirit. *A Vow Fulfilled* is a tribute to the immortality of our people and represents the genre of books necessary for our generation to read. In a world searching for meaning, Fran shows us that contentment is often achieved through selfless acts of kindness, and that our self-worth is not to be measured by profit but rather by social purpose.

Rabbi Kenneth Brander
Dean
Yeshiva University

Young Israel of Scarsdale
Rabbi Jonathan Morgenstern

As the generation of Holocaust survivors dwindles and their collective voice and individual stories are forgotten, it is with great Jewish pride and affirmation of Jewish continuity that Fran Laufer's book, *A Vow Fulfilled*, has been added to the annals of Holocaust memoirs. I am also brimming with pride that this monumental feat was accomplished by my grandmother, Fran Laufer. Her story is engaging and captivating, while also very real and sobering. Fran lost everything, but she was fueled by an inner strength and emotional courage that is, quite simply, virtually non-existent today in our post-Holocaust generation. We, indeed, stand on the shoulders of giants. Who could conceive that out of the ashes of the Holocaust, beacons of light would emerge. Who would have believed that on the very steps of Bergen-Belsen that imprisoned her, Fran Laufer would be wed and begin her life anew, with a renewed sense of optimism and hope for the future.

Fran Laufer's work is an inspiration to all who recognize the Divine Hand in life's events and the enduring power of the human spirit. For one to be able to channel vitriol into love, and hatred into selfless giving, is truly extraordinary. That is what my grandmother, Fran Laufer, has done in this memoir and continues to do every day of her life.

With great love, respect, and admiration,

Rabbi Jonathan Morgenstern
Rabbi, Young Israel of Scarsdale

Praise for
A Vow Fulfilled

A Vow Fulfilled is beautifully written and completely engrossing. The inspiring story of this heroic woman and her husband is a moving account of the endurance of the human spirit and the power of faith. Fran Laufer is a true woman of valor, and her compelling story will not easily be forgotten. *A Vow Fulfilled* should have a profound impact on the hearts and minds of all those who read it, hopefully, for many generations to come.

Pamela Brier
President, Maimonides Hospital

Fran Laufer was put on earth to fulfill a mission. She has done this every day of her life. She has suffered pain and tragedy that is unspeakable. She has also enjoyed the beauty of a wonderful husband, three beautiful daughters and many, many grandchildren and great-grandchildren. Most of all, she has lived her life the way it was meant to be — giving to others and doing for others — in a way that has come to making her the remarkable woman that she is today.

Susan Mascitelli
Vice-President Patient Services
Columbia Presbyterian Hospital

Fran Laufer's *A Vow Fulfilled* is a tribute to the resilience of the human spirit. It is a remarkable, uplifting story about Fran and her late husband, Simon, who were married at the Bergen-Belsen DP camp. Despite their experiences during the Holocaust, the Laufers spent their lives honoring their heritage and their faith through charity, compassion, and love.

David Marwell, Ph.D.
Director of the Museum of Jewish Heritage —
A Living Memorial to the Holocaust

This book is dedicated to the memory of
my dear husband, Simon Laufer.

It is also dedicated to the unforgettable memory of
my dearest parents and siblings,
Zlatte (Lotte) and Shlomie Fuchsbrumer, Itzchak
Dov, and Golda,
and my husband's parents,
Mindel and Sholem Laufer
and his family, who perished in the Holocaust.

Dedicated as well to my dearest children,
Lottie Morgenstern,
Suzie Rozner, and Gayle Yashar.

And to my grandchildren and great-grandchildren:
Cindy Pinter, Daniel and David Rozner,
Lauren Zuckerman,
Dr. Shlomo Morgenstern,
Rabbi Jonathan Morgenstern,
Yocheved Schwartz, Jeremy Yashar, and
Jaclyn Glicksman.

זכור – אל תשכח!
 Remember, don't forget!

Contents

Acknowledgments

I would like to extend my gratitude to the following people:

My dear family for their encouragement, and for helping me bring this book to a successful conclusion.

Rabbi Yisroel Edelman, Rabbi Dr. Sol Roth, Philip Sieradski, Julius Berman, Aryeh Mezei, and Lorri Hershenov.

Avigail Sharer, Bassi Gruen, Allison Fried, and the staff of Targum Press.

Foreword

The title of this book, *A Vow Fulfilled*, speaks volumes about the life of its author. Fran Laufer is inspired by that which is sacred, and she conducts her life in a manner that is appropriately described as fulfilling a sacred vow.

Sanctity belongs to that which instills a sense of reverence. There is a form of appreciation directed at objects of art — a painting, a piece of literature, a musical masterpiece — and a variety of appreciation inspired by that which is holy. The latter is identical to the experience of reverence. A beautiful object is pleasurable for the one who exposes himself to it. Indeed, mankind's pursuit of pleasure is the *raison d'être* of art. On the other hand, the experience of reverence is not one of pleasure, it is rather a form of satisfaction rooted in the knowledge that one has a relation with Him who is of infinite value.

Fran Laufer has an extraordinary capacity for appreciation.

For a good portion of her life she was engaged professionally with interior decoration, bringing beauty into the homes of those who valued her aesthetic talents; indeed, my wife and I were the gratified recipients of her skills. But what is of much greater significance, is that she has an extraordinary capacity for reverence. Her commitment to the sacred was dramatically displayed on the steps of a concentration camp when, together with Simon, the man who became her husband, she took the vow which she complied throughout her life: to live in accordance with the Torah. She lived a life not only of appreciation and beauty, but of reverence and sanctity.

Fran Laufer made a vow to live by Torah precepts when she emerged from World War II. It was not merely an act of defiance against the Nazis, but a positive, unconditional resolve to lead a Torah life. And she demonstrated it equally by her unselfish and dedicated labor on behalf of those who are ill, through her tireless leadership in the Rivkah Laufer Bikur Cholim Society, and via her energetic initiatives on behalf of many Torah institutions.

The story of the life of Fran Laufer will inevitably instruct and inspire. It should be read by all.

Rabbi Dr. Sol Roth
Rabbi Emeritus, Fifth Avenue Synagogue
New York, 2007

Introduction

Sixty-two years ago there was a miracle. As I stood under the wedding canopy in Bergen-Belsen and my new husband asked me what kind of life we would choose to live, in that solemn and blessed moment we decided to adhere to tenets of the Torah and the *mitzvos*. We committed ourselves to continuing the ways of our ancestors, so that what had gone before would not disappear. We promised to raise our children in Torah-true fashion, and we kept that promise to our martyred families.

And now, there is another miracle. Today there are three generations of my life's flesh and blood all celebrating life. *Bli ayin hara*, I have lived to reap beautiful *nachas* from them. From generation to generation, they have remained committed to the path of our ancestors and have not forsaken the Torah. I am humbled, and I thank God.

I thank my children and their families, their teachers, and everyone who made this possible.

And to Simon...words cannot express all that you were to me and what you made possible.

Chapter 1

Chrzanow

In the beginning there was darkness, and G-d created light, and it was good. And then came the sky and the oceans and the land, and these too were good. But then came man, and from man has come not only good but evil. Thus, into each life comes the eternal battle between good and evil, the good and evil that we ourselves do and the good and evil that is done to us.

My story speaks of good — of love, of family, of happy times — and it speaks of the greatest evil that ever befell mankind. It also speaks of living through that evil, overcoming its aftermath, and once again bringing good back to this world. I welcome you to my life.

I was born Frimet (Frimciu) Fuchsbrumer in Chrzanow, Poland, into a middle-class family in what was thought a very

Chrzanow

secure world. As a little girl, I had no idea how hated we Jews were and how my life — and the lives of the innocent people around me — would be devastated in a few short years.

My father, Shlomo, was a chassid, a follower of the Kielcer Rebbe. As there was no Kielcer *shtiebl* in Chrzanow, he davened in the Radomsker shul. Typical of chassidim, he had a full beard and wore a *shtreimel* and *bekeshe* on Shabbos. Because we were from a family with long-established roots in the community, when the Rebbe came to town he would sometimes stay at our home, in a building that had belonged to our family for generations.

My mother Zlata (Lotta) was a women of great intelligence and compassion, and she made our home the joy it was during my youth. Mamishe (as we called her) spoke and read a perfect German and was fluent in both Polish and Yiddish. She could read Hebrew and Yiddish, and she knew how to pray.

My brother Benek was two years younger than me. He was named for both my grandfathers, Berl and Yitzchak, who died long before either of us were born. My sister Golda (Goldzia), named for our paternal great-grandmother, was five years younger than me.

Before 1939, Chrzanow was a fairly large town of about 18,000 people, a third of whom were Jewish. There were two very large synagogues and thirty-nine small *shtieblach* scattered throughout the city.

Chrzanow is located between Krakow and Oswiecim, not far from the German border. The town's main industry was building locomotives. As a border town, however, it was a main transfer area, frequented by many salesmen, and where fruit brokers, wholesalers and tailors operated their businesses. The tailors of Chrzanow were so adept in their craft that demand for their work spread throughout Europe. A vibrant, commercial area, the city was always full of people doing business, craftsmen plying their trades, and a marketplace that was brimming with activity, especially each Thursday morning.

The Jews of Chrzanow were primarily merchants and shopkeepers, butchers, and bakers. In all, it was a well-integrated Jewish community, one that was proud of its sophistication, its piety, and especially its rabbis and scholars.

Mamishe, my mother, was raised in an ultra-Orthodox family. Since Polish children, even Jewish ones, were required to go to public schools, they put up little resistance. In 1898, my mother was listed as one of the most outstanding Polish students in second grade.

My maternal grandfather, Berl Goldberg, owned a number of buildings around town and had a respectable income. He also had a leather business, selling hides for bags, shoes, and other leather goods. The business was housed in one of the buildings he owned, and my parents lived in a large apartment

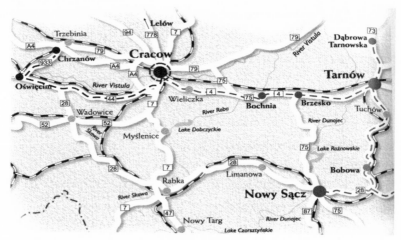

A local map of Poland

in the same building, the apartment in which I was born.

My mother was the youngest of eight — four girls and four boys. Mamishe's sisters married and moved out of the house, but Mamishe was in no rush to marry. She knew that my grandfather needed her to work with him in his business. My grandmother had died at a relatively young age and so my mother took care of her father's needs, refusing to marry until he died. When she finally did marry Shlomo Fuchsbrumer, my father, she was twenty-eight years old — in those days considered old for a young woman but, then again, she had been the youngest child and her primary loyalty had been to her father.

I have no idea how my parents met or who made the match, but I can attest to the fact that my mother's age did not impact on her mothering except in a positive way. After their wedding, my parents opened a retail shoe store on the first floor of the building in which they lived and turned the business into a very prosperous one. In doing so, they incurred the wrath of her siblings who still lived in town. Why? Because when my grandfather died, my mother inherited her father's apartment and lived rent-free above the store!

For years, my mother's brothers and sisters refused to talk to her — except for her sister Mindel, married to David Engelberg. And the reason for their standoffishness was not that they were doing poorly and that my parents didn't care about them. Her oldest sister, Chana Esther, and her husband, Lipa Diamant, owned a printing factory. Itche, the bachelor, took over my grandfather's leather business and was successful, but still resented my mother. He devoted himself to his work until the war broke out. My mother had another brother, Shmuel, who was a jeweler with a shop in Chrzanow. He was married to Anna. Surcie and her husband, Chaim Applebaum, were childless and had a lingerie shop right next door to my parents' shoe store. Surcie was so jealous of my parents that in 1938, she opened up a shoe store right next door to ours, carrying better quality women's and children's shoes than we did. Even I, as a child of thirteen, was upset.

I know my father, my *Tatishe*, came from a smaller town, Jaworzno, about thirty miles from Chrzanow. He had three brothers, Yaakov, Pinchas and one whose name I don't know, who went to live somewhere in South America long before the war. My father also had sisters: Sarah owned a candy store; Chana married Baruch, a *shochet*; and Chava and her husband, Pinchas, lived on

Fran's mother's sisters, Surcie and Chana Esther, at the Krynica spa, 1938

the outskirts of Pechnik, and had a well-run supermarket decades before supermarkets were the norm. They lived in a beautiful house with gardens, where I was sent every summer for a week or two. I really enjoyed myself during those vacations. Though I was the youngest of my cousins by a year or two, we got along very well.

(Years ago, Baruch and Chava's grandson, Meyer Zeiler, was newly married when the Lubavitcher Rebbe told him to move to Israel. He told him to open a fabric factory in Kiryat Malachi and employ the Georgian Jews who were then arriving from Russia. Meyer followed the Rebbe's instructions. For several years he and his family lived in a small apartment where some of the children were born. Finally, he was able to get a permit to build a house. As the Rebbe had indicated, Meyer was very successful in his venture. Today he is a prominent businessman, and many of his children have built their homes next door. The factory has become a major supplier and exporter of specialized fabrics.)

A wedding aufruf, 1938. The Diamant family is celebrating the wedding. The groom is sitting on the right surrounded by his family. Chana Esther Diamant was my mother's sister.

Until recently, our house in Chrzanow and the main square where it was located were still recognizable. The three-story building, which was of no particular style, was located at Rynek 5. (When I met my future husband, Simon Laufer, I discovered our neighbor/family friend, who lived next door at Rynek 7 was in fact Simon's grandfather.) The building was arranged around an outdoor courtyard that was accessed through an alley. The shoe store was the first on a row of shops that faced the square on the right side of the alley. The showcase window was above the entrance to Sender Holtz's food shop, which sold imported delicacies: almonds, herbs, oranges, dried fruit, and other exotic treats. The last store in the row was my aunt's lingerie and notions shop. On the left side of the alley was a fabric store and a menswear shop.

The Rynek served as part of the main hub for the entire region. With buses running from there to all the surrounding towns, the street was always busy. In its prime location, our family's shoe store was visible from a distance.

The Bobover *shtiebl* was located on a street across from the far side of our courtyard. Since people walked through the property to get to services, there was always lots of foot traffic around the shoe store. The store also had a back door that came in handy when people wanted to shop in the evenings or on Sundays, at times when the law demanded that shops stayed closed. Today, they have modernized the square, so it is harder to recognize. In addition, after the war, the townspeople

The Great Synagogue of Chrzanow

destroyed the town's two main synagogues that were located on the side streets along the square.

There as electricity in some places, gaslight in others, and in the days before the war, what is now the central fountain used to be the town's central water pump, where everyone would come with their buckets. Each day people would congregate around the pump and talk about what was happening in town. Our maid, Maria, or a *wassertreger* (a water carrier), would bring the water up to the apartment every day.

Our family lived on the first floor of this large building, up a flight of stone stairs that had a black, wrought-iron railing. Aunt Surcie's apartment was at the top of the stairs and ours was to the right. There was no electricity in our building yet, but there was gaslight, and so we were able to climb the stairs even when it was dark outside. We used coal for cooking and kerosene for additional lighting. When we finally arrived in America, people asked us if we had ever seen or tasted bananas, and if we knew how toilets and light switches worked. It was almost insulting. I can say that in Chrzanow people definitely knew what bananas were and how they tasted, and we had electricity and running water, as well. We may not all have had flush toilets, but we knew how to work them.

At the top of the stairs, on each of the three floors, there was a door that led to an outdoor gallery, similar to a porch. It ran the whole length of the back of the building to the two latrines for the apartments on those floors. My Uncle Itche, who lived on the second floor, had installed a complete modern bathroom. We were in the process of modernizing our apartment when the war broke out.

Our apartment was considered one of the best in the building. It consisted of two large rooms, and you entered directly into a yellow-painted kitchen. There, in the middle of the

Fran with her cousins, July 1939

room, sat a table. Along the far wall there was a bed. The room was big enough for us to put on plays for our schoolmates when we wanted to raise money to buy challahs for a few poor people in town. We would string a curtain across the width of the room and present ourselves for the admission fee of twenty groshen. A wood- and coal-burning stove was on the right, and on the left wall there was a credenza with wooden doors. It was far enough from the wall for me to create a special hiding place for the sandwiches my mother made me which I refused to eat. I didn't want to eat because though people said being plump, or *zaftig*, was stylish, I was twelve and preferred to look chic and thin. I also believed, for some reason I now know is correct, that thinner is healthier. Maria, the maid, would save me from discovery and the wrath of my parents by taking the sandwiches out of their hiding place whenever it seemed likely that they would be discovered.

The one time I did get caught, my parents were furious. They yelled at me for quite some time and I got so upset I ran out of the apartment, through the back of the house, and into a meadow not far from the Bobover *shtiebl*. There, I sat down in the grass and started to cry. I stayed there for more than six hours. Though I was hungry and tired, I was too embarrassed and guilt-stricken to go back home.

As dusk approached and the city began to close down for the night, I thought that I was probably causing my parents additional aggravation, and I didn't want to do that. Finally, I picked myself up and walked back to the house. It turned out that my parents were indeed worried about me, and they were delighted when I walked through the door. That did not mean that I never hid my sandwiches again. It meant that I was more careful and Maria continued to protect me.

Concerned about proper nutrition, my mother worked hard to prepare our food, making everything from scratch. She even plucked the chickens herself when she brought them home from the butcher, and cleaned them and made them kosher. Kitchen work was hard and took all day. But to top it all off, my mother also worked in the shoe store. I attribute my ability to survive to the fact that my mother was such a remarkable role model and an expert on nutrition.

From the three windows in the main room of the apartment, I could look out at the whole town and see my Aunt Mindel's leather store, as well as the rest of the shops along the square. I could watch the May Day parade on May 1, and on May 3 watch the events and parades celebrating the Polish national holiday commemorating the constitution, which was established in 1794. There was always something going on.

The second room in the apartment did triple service. It was our family bedroom and held five beds, a chaise lounge, some tables, extra chairs, and a large armoire. Whenever Mamishe baked cookies, she would put the trays on top of the armoire to cool, and we would sneak a snack when we could. The room, which was very sunny, also served as a guest room and dining room.

• • •

My father's parents were Frimet and Yitzchak, and they had their own leather goods store in Jaworzno. My father's whole family tried their hands at different businesses, but not all of them succeeded as well as my parents did. Some of my aunts and uncles did even better than my parents, because, it is said, they were inspired by their grandmother.

My paternal great-grandmother, Golda Wachsman, was the entrepreneurial type. In 1850, she decided to open what they called in those days a *trafik*, a tobacco shop. But in order to open a store one needed a permit from Kaiser Franz Josef (1830-1916), the ruler of Austria, in whose kingdom Jaworzno then belonged.

Traveling to Vienna from Jaworzno was not simple: The trains didn't run on time and a ticket cost lots of money. One also needed papers to cross borders, and they were difficult to obtain. But Great-Grandma Golda was determined to have her way. She announced to her sons that she intended to see the Kaiser to ask for the concession and, furthermore, they were going to take her there.

The family legend says that her sons — my grandfather and his brothers — bundled her into a wheelbarrow and literally pushed her all the way to the Kaiser's castle in Vienna, a trip that took weeks. Once

My grandmother and namesake Frimet Fuchsbrumer's headstone in Jaworzno, my father's birthplace. (Mrs. Sontag from Jaworzno found my grandmother's headstone in the Jaworzno cemetery and gave me this picture.)

there, she had her audience with the Kaiser and appealed to his kinder instincts. He granted her the tobacco license and, weeks later, she triumphantly came back to town to open her shop on the main street. Later, when her children disagreed with her or dismissed her opinions, she would retort, "*Oy, vey iz mir. Tzim Kaiser Franz Yosef hob ich yoh gekent redden, aber mit meine eigene kinder ken ich nisht redden.*" ("Oh, woe is me. I was perfectly capable of carrying on a conversation with Kaiser Franz Josef but I can't have a conversation with my own children!")

My parents, as I said before, had a shoe store. During the week my father would travel to different cities to buy stock, mostly in Kielce, Sosnowice, and Zarki.

Ours was a family-oriented shoe store, not high-style or high-end. The women's and children's shoes were reasonably priced, because most of our customers were peasants and workers. The women had a variety of styles to choose from, from high heels to flats and oxfords. They could choose from black patent leather or plain black and brown. The children's shoes were mostly high-topped and came in two colors — black and brown. When some people came to buy their children shoes, they would leave the youngest child at home and bring a stick that was cut to the size of the child's foot. We would insert the stick into a shoe and if the measurement fit, the pair was purchased.

Our specialty was a line of men's shoes that my father bought from his uncle, who manufactured high-quality shoes in Jaworzno. These were bought primarily by our Jewish clientele, who were willing to pay for the higher-quality product. Since winters in our part of Europe were particularly harsh, with heavy snow and rain, and many of the roads were unpaved, especially in the small villages of our region, snow shoes and galoshes were also good sellers.

The store had shoes lined up in their boxes on three walls, including the wall behind the bench where customers would sit to try on shoes. For some reason, behind the main wall that faced the front of the store, my father had also built a false wall and stored a hidden inventory of shoes there. At one end of the counter was a clever intercom — a pipe that extended upstairs to our apartment.

In the winter of 1938, my father had an attack of appendicitis and had to be taken to the hospital in Krakow. At the age of thirteen, I took over the store. I was also the sales lady and managed to do a good business in galoshes. Fortunately, our neighbor's sons came and helped me out as well.

My cousin, Chaim Fuchsbrumer, who served as a rabbi in post-war Chrzanow before he made aliyah, told that his father, Yaakov, was a leather dealer in Jarwozno. He did well and, in 1939, he paid to have a *sefer Torah* written. He invited his rabbi, the Krimelever Rebbe, to come and celebrate the giving of the Torah to his shul. His Rebbe refused, saying that the eve of the destruction of the Jews isn't the right time to celebrate. Instead, my uncle gave the Torah to a trusted non-Jewish neighbor, a man named Ruderski, who kept it safe throughout the war and returned it to the family when the war was over. The Torah was brought to Israel and welcomed with a big celebration to the Schinever *shtiebl* in Tel Aviv in the early 1950s.

• • •

My birthday falls on Pesach and my birthday present was invariably a new pair of shoes and a new dress for the holiday, usually with some extra little gift — like an orange or a bunch of grapes, or even a banana. Of course, everyone got new things for Pesach: my sister got a pair of shoes and a dress, and my brother got shoes and a suit. We did not get a lot, but what we did get was always of the finest quality.

We had so much love and respect for our parents, especially my mother, that though they were still relatively young, we wouldn't even allow them to bend down to pick something up from the floor. And our respect was well-rewarded. Every summer my mother would take us on vacation to one of two places. There was a *kuchalein* (a bungalow) in Alwernia or the upscale hotel called "Rabka" in the mountains, where children were the center of attention and everything was geared to them. My mother really believed in catering to her children's needs, and she always made us her first priority. Once, for instance, I became so sick with a high fever that she rushed me to the main hospital in Krakow. There, they discovered that I had chicken pox. They had to decontaminate the entire hospital. And in Rabka she made sure I got inhalation therapy, because the doctors in Krakow had recommended it.

When I was still a preschooler, I already knew that I didn't want to be a woman who spent her time in the kitchen. I would go downstairs and stay in the store, developing a taste for the business. I was told stories about customers, about unusual incidents and, when I was a little older, taught how to transact business. Sometimes my father would get frustrated when customers could not be pleased, or when the gendarmes would threaten to punish my parents when the store was open when it wasn't supposed to be. My mother would say, "What will be, will be, but they won't hang me." Little did she know what was awaiting the Jews of Poland.

They related one story about the marketplace in the square. There, unscrupulous peddlers sold peasants fancy suits for going to church. These *gonifs* (thieves) would sell suits at a price higher than the retail value by putting five zlotys into a suit pocket. When a peasant tried on the suit and found the money, he would think he was pulling a fast one on the vendor and would buy the suit immediately.

There was one Jewish woman who had a dress shop near us who had her own way of doing business. She would give a customer the price of a dress, expecting to haggle over the amount. If the customer did not bargain and asked her to wrap it to go, this woman wouldn't forgive herself for not asking for a higher price in the first place. She actually made herself sick over it. That is how much bargaining was part of our culture.

In the mornings I went to public school. Mamishe would wake us up at about seven, upon which we would wash up and get dressed. We didn't have uniforms, but I had two outfits that I would switch from day to day. I also learned to knit a navy blue cardigan and trimmed its collar with pink angora. We washed up in the kitchen, where Mamishe would serve

Public School class, 1938. (Fran is fourth from the left in the 3rd row.)
Few of these classmates survived the war.

us delicious buttered kaiser rolls and a glass of milk.

During the winter, we were forbidden to drink cold water or eat ice cream. My mother was of the opinion that drinking and eating cold foods in the winter would create the risk of lowered resistance to disease. Avoidance was her way of preventing illness. But the ban on ice cream didn't prevent us from getting other sweets. Benek was a fussy eater and would aggravate my mother, who would bring him to the best bakeries to tempt him to eat. He would sometimes agree to a mini-cheese Danish that I can tell you from personal experience was scrumptious. I used to be a bit jealous of the extra attention his appetite earned him, but as I said, I also did not want to become *zaftig*.

When I was in public school, I would grab my books and walk the two short blocks to the school, where the teachers would lead the class in a Catholic prayer and the Jewish children would keep quiet. There were about 40 girls in each class, about half of them Jewish. The teachers would cover mathematics, Polish history, spelling, grammar, and comparative religion, which was taught in a secular manner by a male Jewish teacher. By one o'clock in the afternoon, we would be done. I'd go home, do my homework in the store and then help out until three o'clock, when I would leave for the local Bais Yaakov.

Before the twentieth century, girls generally did not receive formal schooling, for what need did they have of skills other than cooking, cleaning, and sewing? This was especially true of observant Jews.

Up until the twentieth century, Jews were often banned admission to gymnasiums, universities, and the like, thus isolation — and its accompanying protection from non-Jewish influences — was enforced almost as much by external means as internal ones. Around the turn of the twentieth century, however, things started to change in Europe. Admittance to secular establishments became more common as political and cultural change were on the rise. As a result, people started to rebel. Religious youth began discarding their traditional garb, cutting their hair, reading secular literature, and tasting the forbidden fruit so prevalent outside of their insular lives.

Friends from Bais Yaakov, 1938. Zosia Kling Ramer (1st row, left), Chana Kanner (1st row, right), Lucka Lieblich (3rd row, right), Tobka Klapholz (3rd row, middle), and Frieda Gartner (3rd row, left) are the only ones I know who survived the war.

This was more of a problem for girls than boys, because boys went to *cheder* and yeshivahs and were exposed to formalized tradition and intellectual knowledge. They were able to filter these new influences through their learning. Girls, however, did not have this capability. Until then, it had been enough for them to absorb whatever they could about Jewish law, outlook, and philosophy from the household. Now, though, with more external influences than before, many opened themselves to the exciting new things, threatening the Orthodox Jewish lifestyle.

Sarah Schenirer sensed the potential adverse results of this "modernity." While taking refuge in Vienna during WWI, she conceived the idea of opening a school to teach girls formal Judaism, as was common for boys. Of course, she met with tremendous opposition; her idea was outrageous and seemed blasphemous. Teach girls how to read, how to write? Let them learn from the holy book? Unheard of!

Finally, it was Schenirer's intervention with the Chofetz Chaim and other rabbis — convincing them of the need to prevent the secularization of observant Jewish females — that formally permitted girls, for the first time, to learn Torah. Schenirer believed that by providing young girls with a Jewish education and then training teachers to take her methods to other cities and towns, she could help combat assimilation.

Dubbed "the chassidis'te" by her family, she founded the Bais Yaakov movement, essentially a *cheder* for girls that would spread throughout Eastern Europe and eventually be transplanted to America and Israel in the aftermath of the Holocaust.

This great lady, who never had children but was mourned by thousands of her "daughters," was of medium height, with dark hair and strong features. She used to come to our school when I was a very young girl, to teach us and to test our knowledge. She stressed the need for us to be charitable young ladies and reminded us how important it is to be kind to the poor and the sick. She would offer us advice on how to give charity so as not to embarrass the recipients. One method she recommended was for us to stick our hands through an unlocked door of an apartment where the poor person lived, and deposit money

Bais Yaakov class, 1939. Fourth and fifth from the left (seated) are Mrs. Blum and Mrs. Wiener. (Fran is third from right, standing.)

in a coat pocket hanging near the open door. I did that once or twice myself.

The Bais Yaakov which I attended from grades one to seven was further away from our house than the public school and in the opposite direction. I had to cross the square and walk four more blocks to a building on a side street. Our class had about twenty students.

Whenever a holiday came, we would review the reasons for the holiday and its rules and regulations. Our teachers were Mrs. Blum and Mrs. Wiener, who taught us *Tanach*, halachah, and *lashon hakodesh*, which is not the same as modern Hebrew. We also studied Hebrew grammar. I really enjoyed the whole experience of going to school and learning. My parents also made sure I learned what they call *handarbeit* (handwork), so that I would know how to delicately stitch lingerie or do needlepoint.

In June 1939, upon graduating from this Bais Yaakov school, I entered the Bnos of the Agudah Yisroel movement.

After I graduated from my regular secular school, I took commercial courses for a year in a co-ed school called the Handlowka, until the war broke out and we were no longer permitted to go to school.

• • •

Just before the war years, the Jewish community in Chrzanow was very expansive and many different kinds of groups joined. There were socialist Jewish movements, secular Zionists, religious Zionists, chassidim, Modern Orthodox, and completely secular Jewish movements — including hard-core communists. Newspapers available in the city included Yiddish papers from all of these groups, though the main Polish/Jewish paper was called *Nowy Dzienik* and the Yiddish papers were *Moment* and *Heint*. Orthodox parents often made all the decisions for their children, to prevent them from lessening their observance or falling, G-d forbid, into assimilation — or even worse, developing an unseemly relationship with a boy.

It was precisely because of the community's expansiveness that I was sent to Bais Yaakov, where they would teach me how to be a good wife and mother who obeyed all the rules, not the least of which was that there was no communication with boys. My parents were very strict about this.

This separation of boys and girls was something that was very important in the religious community, a community that needed to define itself against all these new forms of Judaism that developed after World War I. From my window I often saw boys and girls going to and from activities in groups that I would never be allowed to join, though sometimes I wished I could.

Chesed, charity and kindness, was the pride of our lives. We had boys who were learning in local yeshivahs come eat in our house twice a week, on Tuesdays and Thursdays. The custom was called *essen teg* (eating days), with the boys going to a different house every day.

The mitzvah of *bikur cholim*, taking care of the sick, was also performed enthusiastically. Often, my mother would fill up a *menashke*, a trio of nested pots with a handle, with hot food and soup that I would bring to a patient at the local hospital, where poor people or people who were too sick to go to Krakow, would be brought.

• • •

The busiest days of our week were Thursdays and Fridays. On Fridays, everyone rushed to get everything done by sundown. The *cholent* would be prepared in a big clay pot, wrapped in brown paper and tied with a cord, with the family name scribbled on the paper, and brought to the bakery for cooking overnight. There was an *eruv* that allowed Jews to carry things from one place to another on Shabbos. Sometimes the children who were sent to fetch the pots the next morning would grab a *cholent* that didn't belong to them — they figured that what they took would taste better than their own mothers' cooking.

For those who did not have their own businesses or employment in Chrzanow, work took them to other towns and cities where they labored from Sunday through Friday — and some quite successfully. Friday afternoon they would return home for Shabbos. The train would come in from Katowice — people would yell in the street, "*Der Shabbos Zug is ungekimen* — The Shabbos train has come." Crowds would wait for it in the station, about half a mile from the main square. Children came to greet their fathers; hosts to greet their guests. There was great happiness when the heads of household brought home the *parnassah* for the following week.

On Friday nights and Shabbos morning, my father would put on his *shtreimel* and go to shul. On Shabbos in Chrzanow you couldn't tell who was poor and who was rich, because everyone was dressed in their finest and cleanest clothing. Benek, who at the time was in yeshivah learning Talmud with his *rebbes*, would accompany our father to shul. In addition to learning, Benek was also very handy, and he taught himself to wire things for electricity. This would be useful during the Nazi occupation — at least for a while.

Once the candles were lit on Friday night and the men

came back from shul, often with a guest, Tatishe would sing *zemiros* and make Kiddush, and my mother would serve the meal. After dinner, we would visit other families or they would visit us. In the summertime, candle lighting was much later, so Fridays were not quite as hectic, and socializing was saved for the next day.

Women and girls in our circles customarily didn't go to shul every Shabbos; instead, they davened at home. Mostly, women and girls just went to shul on Rosh HaShanah and Yom Kippur, to pray for forgiveness and hear the blowing of the *shofar*.

The *yamin tovim* were an especially important part of our lives. As part of the High-Holiday preparations, my father would bring chickens in a crate to the house for *shlugging kaporos*, the ritual of swinging a chicken over one's head. Afterward, the chicken would go back to the *shochet* to be slaughtered and we would eat it for the last meal before Yom Kippur. In those days, only the men went to *tashlich* on Rosh HaShanah, not like in America, where everyone goes as a family and it becomes a social event.

On Simchas Torah night we were permitted to watch the men dance in our own synagogues — there was no "shul-hopping" in those days — and on Purim we would go to hear the Megillah. In our family, no one wore costumes on Purim, but we did send *mishloach manos*. We celebrated Chanukah with much joy; my father would light the candles with great ceremony, and we would all sing the Chanukah songs together. My mother would fry up some delicious latkes and we would play *dreidl* and collect Chanukah *gelt*. My husband Simon used to tell me that his grandmother, who lived in Krakow, would come to his house with her *knipl* (a stash of money bound up in a handkerchief) and give all her grandchildren her precious coins.

We also went to shul on Tisha B'Av, the saddest day of the Jewish year. We'd fast and listen to the reading of *Eichah* and *Kinos*, and we would sit on boxes or on the floor to listen. Afterward we would go for a walk, because there was nothing else to do, and the boys would get hold of nettles and throw them into the girls' hair. Why? I have no idea. Maybe they wanted us to suffer on that day, because believe me, pulling nettles out of long hair can be very painful.

On Wednesdays or Thursdays, when I had a minute, I would run over to the library to borrow books to read over Shabbos — children's books when I was younger and, as I got older, books by famous authors, like Sinclair Lewis and Dostoyevsky. I would spend Shabbos morning reading and setting the table with my mother, waiting for my father and Benek to come home. Benek would bring in the *cholent* from the bakery, which was delicious because my mother was a great cook.

Mamishe would also serve carp and white fish; she only made gefilte fish during the war when there was no fresh fish. In the bad days we found some canned tuna on the black market and worked with that, but usually, on Friday night we ate fish, chicken soup with egg barley, and roasted chicken or beef. On Shabbos day, we ate fish,

Afternoon walk on the Plantn in Chrzanow just before the war, Marymka Zolman (Miriam Schneider) and myself

chopped eggs with onion, chopped liver, *cholent*, and a main dish. Dessert would usually be a compote of seasonal fruits, and during the war Mamishe would make a delicious fake cheesecake out of potatoes.

After lunch, especially in the summer, we would go for strolls on the Aleja Henryka — called the Plantn — dressed in our finest clothes, and greet all our friends. We didn't go for these strolls with our parents, just girls with girls and boys with boys. Those who were less religious, in their early teenage years, would hang out together, boys and girls.

Like I said, I was never allowed to mingle with boys, and my parents were alert to every nuance of my growing up. Once, when I let my braids out, my father took one look at me and said, "No. You will not go out of the house looking like that." I rebraided my hair.

There were times I would go out with my friends and I knew my parents would sometimes look out the window to check if I was behaving properly and to make sure I wasn't talking to boys. But I never did anything behind their backs. Their point of view was that there was no point in having anything at all to do with boys...and that was just the way things were.

Chapter 2

The Ghetto

Until the war shattered our illusions, we Jews in Chrzanow were an optimistic people. As a border town, we constantly dealt with the seemingly polite and civilized Germans, who we thought had no problem with Jews. And so we had no idea how terrible they would be after the invasion. It took a while for us to realize that we were being fooled into cooperating with our own deaths, because in our minds we could not imagine that the Germans could do what they were actually doing.

We thought our clients were also our friends, but once the Germans came and anti-Jewish laws were put into place, we found out that no one we knew was a friend at all. In fact, some became collaborators who couldn't wait to tell the Germans who was a Jew or show them where the Jews were hidden.

I was twelve years old, and I remember that September 1, 1939 was a Friday. I woke up and prepared to go to school.

As *Mamishe* made breakfast, the radio announced that war had begun. We looked out the window and saw that everywhere was chaos. People were running through the streets, all looking for a place to escape from the oncoming Nazi war machine.

My parents decided not to open the store that day. They spoke to their relatives in our building and decided that fleeing to Krakow might be a good idea, because it was a bigger city and further away from the border. My Uncle Itche, a very wealthy man, informed us that he had access to a ship. I don't know if he bought it or rented it, but he asked my parents and Aunt Surcie and her husband to join him on the ship and sail to Russian waters and safety. The ship was docked not far from our town. Afraid to leave the store and its contents, my parents said no.

While before the war, the family fought with each other, on that day everything changed. Surcie refused to leave my mother and us alone. So Itche, the bachelor, ran to his boat and took off for Lemberg, where the Russians soon after got control. He survived and lived in Paris after the war. I am certain that had we gone with him, our whole family would have survived the war.

My mother came into the apartment after the family conference and told us to get ready to go to Krakow, where she and my father felt they would blend in more and not be as noticeable to the Germans. I was in my bedroom with my sister Goldzia, who was then about eight years old. We knew we couldn't carry anything with us, and we also knew that during the night we would be exposed to the already markedly cooler weather. Benek was told to wear double layers of clothing. I wore two dresses and so did Goldzia. My mother also packed some food for us.

Because my mother had bunions and other foot trouble — her shoes had to be custom-made — she would not be able to travel to Krakow with us by foot. And so, we needed to find a method of transportation for her. Since very few people had cars or trucks, little thought was given to obtaining some sort of motorized vehicle. Fortunately, we were able to hire a horse and buggy to take *Mamishe* to Krakow, where she would meet us at the home of Surcie's in-laws, the Dubiner family. They had a large apartment in the center of town and made their money manufacturing cardboard boxes and renting out storage space.

When the horse and buggy took off with my mother, we began to walk the thirty miles to Krakow. It was still light when we left: my father, Benek, Goldzia, Surcie and her husband Chaim, and I. My father, then fifty years old, was already feeling his age. I had imagined, until that night, that my father was the strongest man in the world; I had never seen him falter. But before the night was over, Benek and I were helping him walk; we had to hold him upright so that he wouldn't stumble and fall.

We walked out of our town on the main road, which was really a country road lined with woods on each side, with an occasional farm or estate visible in the distance. We didn't see a soul on any of the properties. But the road was quite different. We were not the only ones trying to get away from the German border. It was very frightening and chaotic. Many of our fellow-escapees were Polish soldiers fleeing the German troops. People were so scared and overwhelmed that we all remained silent or spoke in whispers. All we heard was footsteps shuffling on the road. We were too scared to be hungry or thirsty. The people around us were all headed in the same direction: to Krakow. To safety, we thought, in a larger city.

It took all night and more than half of the next day to get there. We arrived at the Dubiner home, a very large building in the center of the city with impressive wooden doors, and a big *mezuzah* on the gate. We opened it and went to the first floor, where we found the Dubiners and my mother.

Deportation, February 1943

My mother greeted us with great relief. We were all thrilled that nothing had happened to any of us on this trip, though we knew that the future was uncertain and extremely dangerous. We could never imagine what would follow.

On September 4, 1939, the Germans marched into Chrzanow.

For the next two weeks, we were always together in the apartment in Krakow, not believing that there was a war going on. From the apartment window, everything looked so normal. Though we listened to the radio, there was never any news, nothing that could have helped us. Also, listening to the radio was forbidden by the Germans, and so we listened and hoped we wouldn't be caught.

A few days later, I looked out of a window and watched the German army march into the city, their boots making an awful sound as they hit the sidewalks. The Germans looked huge, a symbol of terrifying power. My parents felt that if the Germans were already everywhere, they didn't want to impose on the Dubiners any longer, and they decided to return home.

My father, however, with his long beard, thought he would be safer and less visible in Krakow. Chaim stayed with him. My parents rented a horse and buggy for my mother and the rest of us and sent us back to Chrzanow.

When we approached Trzebinia, about fourteen miles from home, a Polish peasant woman met us along the way and warned us that the Germans were slaughtering the Jews in Trzebinia and throwing their bodies into a pit near the monastery. The victims were the men who had fled Chrzanow on the first day of the war and were now making their way back. Among them were young men who were my neighbors. They were the first people who I knew that were killed in the war.

For some reason, that peasant woman had helped us. We don't know why she didn't report us to the Germans, as many of her neighbors were doing. For us, she was a guardian angel who certainly prevented us from being killed that day.

We now made our way directly to Chrzanow. As we neared, we heard how the Germans had taken Poles and Jews prisoner the week before and then, just as inexplicably, let them go. We also heard that the train station in Trzebinia had been bombed and that food shortages were already serious.

Looking back, each day was a horrific experience, and we thought it couldn't get worse than it was that particular day. But it always did get worse.

When we finally arrived home, we discovered that our shoe store had been looted. There were shoes all over the floor — left feet, right feet, without a pair. There had obviously been a frenzy of people grabbing whatever they could. The majority of the stock was now gone, the store's windows broken, and the furniture wrecked. The vandals who had broken into the store had stolen hundreds of pairs of shoes, but luckily, they did not find the shoes my father had hidden behind the false wall.

Surcie, who just a few months before had not been on speaking terms with us, saved the day. For some reason, her shoe store had not been broken into. Saying "what's mine is yours," she offered to merge our two stores. And that's how we continued to survive in the early days of the war.

My father came back to Chrzanow a week later. We were terrified for him because the Germans were torturing Jews who wore beards — cutting off their beards and *payos* in the middle of the street. I had seen them do it. But my father still refused to shave. Sometimes he would wrap a scarf around his face to hide his beard, but every time he walked out into the streets he risked his very life.

As days lapsed into weeks and then into months, there was a daily appropriation of people for labor details. Whether in the middle of the day or the middle of the night, you'd hear the sound of boots in the streets, running up steps, pounding on doors, and grabbing whoever they wanted for their work details. Every day people would pray to see their loved ones again, never knowing if indeed that would happen.

In addition to grabbing people, the Germans also grabbed whatever they could get their hands on. Everything was being confiscated. Staples and commodities like soap, oil, flour, and sugar were quickly seized. Just before the war, my Aunt Mindel and her husband, David Engelberg, had invested in buying supplies and storing them in the cellar of the house in which they lived on Krzyska Street and in their leather goods shop. One morning, the Germans showed up with their trucks and took everything. Thank G-d, Mindel and her husband were not shot. (It had become the German practice that if someone was found with fresh food, like eggs or butter, he was beaten or shot.)

The German head of the police was a sadistic man by the name of Schindler, who enjoyed making our lives even more difficult. One of his practices was to pretend to be a friend of the Jews, taking bribes from those caught in his web, and then make himself *nisht wissendig* (unknowing) of those who had bribed him when they came to him in need.

And so we came to understand terror and how it worked — intimidating and demoralizing us so that we would never think of resisting the Germans. They did whatever they wanted to us.

On October 6, the Germans surrounded the town and went on a house-to-house search for loot, breaking into stores and taking anything, including the smallest scraps of food from the poorest Jews. It was organized theft of the worst sort, and it further demoralized the Jews of Chrzanow.

With all the food taken by the Germans, people began to starve. People waited on bread lines and began to beg in the streets. That made them targets for German troops wandering through the town. We were told how the rabbi's deaf son was shot for not hearing the Germans who were ordering him to stop, and how they were about to execute fifteen more men who came to bury the poor boy, when a German officer discovered what was happening and, for some reason, prevented them from doing so.

The *Jüdenrat* was formed at the end of 1939, but it was the tool of the Germans and provided them with whatever they asked for: from money (under the guise of tax payments) to coffee, sugar and other staples, to bodies for slave labor. Administered by corrupt and terrible people, the only useful thing the *Jüdenrat* did was to open a soup kitchen and bury the dead martyrs from Chrzanow who had been slaughtered in Trzebinia in the first week of the war.

We watched as Jews were tortured and held hostage. The Germans forced all kinds of false confessions from people and had people bear false witness against each other in order to prevent their own families from being slaughtered. The Germans, who worked with Poles willing to betray their former neighbors, killed many people for the "crimes" committed by "one" person, teaching us a lesson in something called "collective responsibility." Paying bribes to Poles and Germans was a common and necessary practice among those who tried to survive.

Every day they stepped on our pride and dignity, but that was just the beginning. Each day there were new announcements, new restrictions; even the streets of the city were closed to us — and sidewalks were not for the Jews. They confiscated our apartments and our furniture and moved people from their homes into crowded ghettos, where many families were squeezed into tiny places. Because people didn't want to part with the goods that they had accumulated through the years, they paid with their lives for the small suitcases and the few personal belongings that they tried to keep with them. Whether a silver candlestick or simple family photographs — it made no difference. The Germans took everything. They took gold, silver, radios, dinnerware, furniture — anything that made us feel like humans was taken away.

And then came the order to wear a white band with a Jewish star on our right arms, and that really prevented us from moving around anymore. This was supposed to bring us shame, because every German soldier — many of them just young boys — took it upon themselves to beat and push and hit and kick anyone they saw wearing a white band.

Little by little, the Germans whittled away at our dignity until there was almost none left. We wanted to resist, but it was hopeless. Those who tried were shot on the spot. We could only hope that if we did what they wanted us to do they would let us live. Our desire to live was deep and abiding.

• • •

In 1940, Chrzanow was incorporated into the Third Reich and cut off from Krakow. Trzebinia became a border town and Jews had to pay huge bribes to German officials if they sought to continue their businesses and travel to and from local markets. Young Jews, realizing that a Nazi noose was being tied around their community, decided to risk their lives and cross into Russian territory by swimming across the San River. Those who survived the trip also managed to survive the war.

Despite it all, for us 1940 was a fairly normal year, considering how terrible things were. The thugs who ran the local *Jüdenrat* were replaced with decent people, like Betzalel Cuker, Mendl Nussbaum, and Moyshe Nagashiner, who earnestly sought to make their fellow Jews' lives somewhat more bearable. Though whatever they tried could not remove the heavy hand of German rapaciousness, they nevertheless tried to make their fellow Jews' burdens easier. For instance, in order to prevent the rampant kidnapping of people for labor details, the *Jüdenrat* began to act as a sort of employment agency, delivering slave laborers to the Germans. Everyone had to work at slave labor at least one day a week or pay a fee to the *Jüdenrat* to have them supply a replacement.

Because the Germans were so greedy and corrupt, by paying

the necessary bribes people were also able to buy permits to reopen their stores, thereby trying to resume some semblance of normalcy. Such was this normalcy that many German Jews also began moving into the town, though they angered many of the residents as they were treated better than the "natives" because of their German connections.

Then, on Simchas Torah, after they had let us *daven* in the *shtieblech* for Rosh HaShanah and Yom Kippur, the Great Schul and the Mizrachi shul, the Germans took hundreds of young people and married men to work in slave labor camps, forcing them to work on roads in the bitter winter months. Because feeding or sheltering them properly was not on the German agenda, they died at alarming rates.

My brother and I were not conscripted because our shoe store was taken over by the Germans and handed to non-Jews. But someone had to run the store, and I was given that assignment by our new German masters. An overseer (*troyhandler*) put a Ukrainian girl in charge of me, and between the two of us we managed what was deemed an important service. I was then fifteen years old.

Since the Germans were fastidious in their control of things, every shoe in the store had to be numbered. Everyone who came into the store to buy a pair of shoes needed to have a ration card from the German authorities. A customer would come in, present his ration card and then receive a pair of shoes. But sometimes, as it happened, we would have to special order a pair of shoes and the customer would leave his ration card. (Even if the ration card was not left, my memory was so acute that I recalled the necessary numbers and was thereby still able to acquire shoes for the black market.) Occasionally, that customer never came back. This would give me the opportunity to remove the number from the shoes and sell them on the black market. This was difficult and dangerous, but my family need to survive and so I took the necessary risk.

At the end of the year we were all pushed into a ghetto on the other side of the Plantn and the Rynek, now totally Aryanized. No Jew was allowed anywhere near there anymore. As the Germans liked to say, it was now *Jüdenrein,* free of Jews.

My parents were not allowed to work, and they stayed in the now-tiny apartment in the ghetto we had been forced to occupy. No matter what the Nazis did to us, we still continued to hope that there would be no more depredations. It was a frantic hope, a belief that if we did everything we were told to they would let us live. Such was our will to survive — and the will to delude ourselves.

I was paid a pension once a month with which I was able to buy a little bit of food on the black market. But for the family to live, I was forced to steal, even though what I was stealing was the shoes the Germans had stolen from us. Every week I "organized" two or three pairs of shoes that hadn't been picked up by customers. Whatever I could get my hands on I took and sold on the black market. That's how we got the money to afford food — not to make money, but just to be able to eat. Had I been caught, it would have gotten us all killed.

And so we lived from hand to mouth, my brother and sister, my parents and my aunt, all of us squeezed together into a tiny apartment with an outdoor bathroom that everyone in the area had to stand in line to use. Even so, my mother would not let our schooling lapse. Though we were not permitted to attend school, she managed to hire German and English teachers to tutor her children. For this foresight, I indeed owe her my life.

As the Russians began their advance against the Germans, things became more difficult. The Nazis increased their campaign of tormenting Jewish men in the streets, sending them out to slave labor on the outskirts of the town, beating and abusing them mercilessly.

The summer brought with it occasional acts of terror and some deportations, but in the fall the Germans began to squeeze us into poorer areas, shrinking the ghetto yet again and making sure conditions were extremely crowded — with no food, medicine, water, or basic necessities readily available. Now we were squeezed into a yet smaller apartment on Kadlubek Street.

By November 1941, the Germans began to round up young girls and send them to labor camps, as well as the men. For the moment, however, because I had a *sonderpass,* working papers we were given that allowed us to work in an Aryanized business, I was spared. For Benek and me our *sonderpassen* were priceless, for they constituted life itself. As long as we were considered essential to the German economy, there was hope for another day of life; without them, deportation would certainly follow.

PROTOKOLL

Jews in the ghetto were issued Protokolls, identity cards. This one was for Miriam Laufer, Shimon's sister.

In the first week in March, 1942, there was a big roundup in the market place. The Germans had announced that they were going to distribute extra rations. Of course just about everyone appeared, their hunger was so intense. But, as usual, the Germans lied. In reality, they were looking to loot whatever we had left — furs, coats, any half-decent clothing, jewelry. Any pretext was used to send people to Auschwitz — and to their death.

In April the sun was shining brightly, the trees and flowers starting to bloom. In contrast to this beauty, the Germans once again showed us the ugliness of men. On a day that spoke of new life, the Germans rounded up my parents and some 3,000 other Jews and imprisoned them in the local schoolhouse. Separating husbands from wives, children from parents, brothers from sisters, the promise of new life was instead a promise of death.

Because of his many dealings with Germans in his jewelry business, my Uncle Shmuel was not among those in this roundup. As soon as he found out that his sister had been taken, through his contacts he located a *macher* to get my parents out. A day or two later, my parents were smuggled out of the school house using a rope ladder dropped from a fourth-floor window.

Deportation by cattle trains

Our joy at my parents' return was great, but it was muted by the fact that all the others the Nazis had rounded up in that school were deported to Auschwitz. Though Auschwitz was not very far

Monument ot the seven hanged martyrs in Chrzanow

away, none of us knew exactly what was going on there — most of us thought it was just a work camp. But even work camps were horrendous, and so we mourned our fellow Jews consigned to whatever fate awaited them there.

Around that time, Israel Gerstner, a Jewish baker, was taken out and hanged. Poles had noticed smoke coming from his chimney and had reported it to the Germans. Six others were condemned for minor infractions and hanged as well. Today, there is a monument to these men in Chrzanow: Israel Gerstner, Chaim Gerstner, Szymszon Gerstner, Szaja Spangelet, Fajwel Waldman and Israel Frisz. Almost 900 people had their identity cards taken away to force them to witness the executions, in yet another classic case of collective punishment by the Germans.

My parents sensed that any *Appell* (roll call) might mean the end and always insisted that Benek, Goldzia, and I find hiding places when the Germans issued their orders. "Hide and live," they would tell us constantly.

It was also about this time that my cousin, Lotka Goldberg (who survived Bergen-Belsen and now lives in Israel), witnessed something she would carry with her for the rest of her life. Living in the town of Rzeszów, some 100 miles east of Krakow, she was assigned to a work detail at local rail yards. One day, when a train arrived, she heard the cries of children coming from the closed cars. Able to peer into the dark interior of a nearby car, Lotka saw young children squeezed one on top of another, all of them crying, all of them looking painfully undernourished. Tiny hands reached out through the cracks in the train walls, begging for any scrap of food. Reaching into her dress, she took out the only thing she had, an apple, and handed it to one child. Suddenly, the train moved. Though the child held onto the apple, the crack was too small to bring the apple into the train. As the train pulled away, indelibly etched in her mind, was the sight of the forlorn child with the apple in his hand trying desperately to get it through the hole.

• • •

One morning, in August of 1942, we woke up to see posters mounted all around, ordering us to the market place. The posters explained that there a need to verify our IDs in order increase our rations. Of course, everyone showed up. Just a few months earlier, the Germans had merged our shoe store with that of a Pole by the name of Bytomsky and moved us to larger quarters. When we saw the posters, instead of reporting, Benek, Goldzia, and I ran to the big shoe store and hid behind the shoe boxes on the extra wide shelves. Luckily, the Ukrainian girl who was working for the Nazis wasn't around that morning. Bytomsky, on the other hand, was a decent man who despised the Germans and resented the fact that they had taken his business away from him as well. He did not report us.

From our hiding place, we watched as everyone who had gathered in the market place was divided into three groups — a group to Auschwitz, a group to slave labor camps, and a group to stay in town.

That day they took all my family — my mother, father, aunts, and uncles — initially to the school and, a few hours later, to waiting trains. Only Uncle Shmuel and Aunt Anna

Goldberg weren't taken, Shmuel's contacts from his jewelry store again helping save him from the rest of the family's fate. There was no time for me to do anything about it. I watched them go from the store window with my heart in my mouth. I felt terribly guilty that I wasn't taken, too.

The marketplace was soon empty and the deportation was over. We came out of our hiding place. I do not remember how this happened, but sometime on that day, after my parents were put on the train, someone saw me and pressed a piece of fabric into my hand. It was a piece of my mother's slip and on it she had written in her own blood, "Hide and live!"

Chapter 3

Deportation

I was now seventeen, alone with my fifteen-year-old brother and my ten-year-old sister. To survive, my brother worked as an electrician, servicing different buildings for the Germans. My sister worked in coal bins and would scrounge and prepare food for us. I continued to work in the shoe store. Each month the Germans would come and tally the receipts from all the shoe stores in the area. I always had the highest tally. They would say, "*Die kleine had record geschlagen*" ("That little one won the contest"), and I would be safe from deportation a while longer. That stamp of approval was priceless — it meant that my ticket to life had, for one month more, been extended.

And so, amid the lies and deadly betrayals that the Nazis propagated daily, life continued for about six more months. The seasons changed, the weather grew bitter, and we were always hungry. But we were alive. Soon, though, even that changed.

On February 18, 1943, my uncle told me of a new rumor that the Germans were about to round up people who worked for the *Troyhandlers* (overseers). I was one of them, and so was my brother. If the rumor was true, our *sonderpassen* that had protected us until this point, had just become worthless and, in fact, would now be our death warrants. We soon discovered, however, that it was just another German ruse. The Germans were not just going after a limited number of Jews, their real goal was to round up all the Jews in Chrzanow and make it *Jüdenrein*.

Not knowing the full extent of the German plans, and in an attempt to thwart their roundup of Jews with *sonderpassen*, my brother went to stay with some cousins, the Stockstiels, who were in charge of a uniform factory for the Nazis. Since we thought they were only looking for *sonderpass* holders and my sister didn't have one, she was left with a neighbor. I was hidden by my aunt and uncle.

In the middle of the night, while huddled in bed, we heard jackboots noisily tromping up the stairs of their building. In the time the Nazis entered the building and broke down the door to their apartment, my aunt and uncle jammed me in between the box spring and the mattress of the bed and then climbed back in. I could breathe only because my face was to the crack between the bed and the wall.

Once the Nazis broke down the door, they dragged my aunt and uncle out into the street in their nightclothes and marched them to the train station. They never bothered looking under the mattress — a miracle all by itself.

As I lay there, overwhelmed by fear, I heard gunshots and dogs barking. My mind raced: What had happened to my aunt and uncle? What would happen to me now? Would the Nazis come back? Terror-filled minutes ticked by. Any minute now, I thought, I would be discovered. And then what?

Slowly the minutes ticked away. One hour, two. And it

became very quiet. I had no idea what would happen next, but I figured that the cellar might be a safer place to hide. Climbing out from behind the mattress, I carefully left the apartment and quietly descended the stairs to the building's basement. (Years later, on a trip to Poland, I showed my grandchildren this cellar.) As unlikely as it would seem, there I found a neighbor, a Mrs. Gross. Her son, Shlamek, one of the most popular boys in the community, was my age. I had noticed him in school, even though I was never allowed to socialize with him beyond saying hello and goodbye.

The cellar was pitch-black, cold, and wet. There was no lighting — not a gaslight, not a candle, not a lantern. In the darkness, all we could make out were the sacks of potatoes stored against the walls, a food supply for those who would now never eat of them.

Feeling our way around the room we discovered that we were the only two people there. Terrified and not knowing what to do, Mrs. Gross told me to wait while she went back to her apartment. When she returned a few minutes later, she had a number of items with her: Shlamek's custom-made, navy-wool winter coat and two designer-quality silk scarves. She told me that as an older person she felt she wouldn't make it through the rest of the war and said that I should take her son's coat and give it to him should I by chance find him. She then gave me the two scarves as a gift. Little did I know that she had just handed me the gift of life.

Expressing my thanks to Mrs. Gross and assuring her that I would do what I could to find her son and tell him of her location, I put on the coat and left the cellar to look for Benek. It was still dark outside and very quiet. Too quiet. I felt as if I was walking in a ghost town. There wasn't a soul in the street; the entire town seemed empty. Besides Mrs. Gross, I felt as if

I was the only Jew still left in Chrzanow.

My brother Benek had gone to the Stockstiels because Moshe Stockstiel was the head of a German shop, and so we thought they had some *protektsia* with the Germans. But when I arrived, there was not a soul to be found. I went into their house. It had been completely ransacked. I ran out and headed in the opposite direction toward the apartment we used to have in the ghetto, thinking that perhaps either my sister or brother would think to meet me there. Alas, not. The building was completely empty of Jews.

There were things that my parents had hidden in the apartment, but before I had the chance to take the silver dollars my father had sequestered in the light fixtures, and before I could put some potatoes and carrots into my pockets, the superintendent's son must have heard me walking around. He burst in with an iron poker and threatened to denounce me. I ran for my life. The only place I could think of to run to was the *Jüdenrat* office, and he chased me for the three long blocks as I ran to get there.

When I burst into the *Jüdenrat* office, three older men were there, along with two women and the chief officer — all amazed that I had survived the round-up. They offered me some food and advised me to stay with them, since going back out onto the streets would be dangerous. For them I was a G-dsend, because a younger person provided them with a chance not to be sent to Auschwitz (the Nazis, needing young labor, would deport us as a group).

Though I was no longer alone, the guilt of losing my brother and sister in this *aktion* overwhelmed me. I had no idea if I'd ever see them again, although I hoped against hope that I would find them, that somehow they would survive. It wasn't until 2004, when I attended a lecture by Aharon

Ahrenfeldt, a historian who reached deep into my soul, that I finally rid myself of the guilt that enveloped me for so many years. He said, "I know that many of you feel guilty for having survived. You should not feel guilty; you were left alive for a reason, an important reason — to prove to the world that Hitler did not achieve his goal and to continue to live and build a future."

Two days later, all of us were on a train, young and old alike. We could see in each others' faces the fear and confusion that tormented our own souls, especially since the train ride took hours and hours instead of the usual hour and a half it would have taken if our destination had been Auschwitz. Looking out the window, we could see bodies — dead and alive — scattered along the tracks. Some people near the tracks took pity on us and threw some food through the windows of the train so we could have something to eat. Still, there was no water.

Finally, the train pulled into a station, the signs indicating that we were in Sosnowice. As the train doors flung open, the squeal of iron on iron was soon replaced with the Germans barking at us, *"Raus, Jüden!"* ("Out, Jews"). They forced us off the train and into waiting trucks. After a short ride, we were told to climb out; we were now in a transit camp, a *Durchgangslager*. They separated the men from the women and assigned us to bunks that lined the rooms of the dormitories in the large complex, hundreds of people jammed into a single room. During the course of the day, people came and went as they were shipped off to different camps.

As I climbed into my designated bunk, I furtively looked around the room to see if there was anyone I knew among the hundreds of men and women there. There was no one I recognized. I still held on to a hope of finding my brother and sister.

In a little while they fed us some bread and ersatz coffee and then let us sleep. The next morning they began assigning people to different work camps. They called my name but I ignored the call, thinking that if I stayed in this *lager* long enough I might somehow find my siblings, or maybe an aunt, an uncle, or a cousin. I don't remember how I managed it on a regular basis, but I avoided being sent out of the camp for three weeks. In all that time, I didn't find anyone I knew.

After those three weeks, those who had initially come with me on the train were long gone for some of the "better" work camps in Czechoslovakia. Though I had been able to avoid being shipped out this whole time, my luck eventually ran out. When my name was once again called, I was finally forced to present myself for assignment. The man handling my paperwork told me that I was going to go to one of the harshest labor camps in the area — and that I wouldn't come out alive. In these camps women did men's work, rigorous labor that even few men survived. They put me on a train to the hell that was to be my new home.

It had to be the middle of March 1943. I found out later that March 10 was the day they'd sealed the ghetto. A week or so later they had killed the remaining members of the *Jüdenrat* from Chrzanow.

• • •

After a four-hour ride, our group arrived in Neusalz (Nowasol), near Breslau, in Upper Silesia. (Today, this area is part of Poland.) As soon as we got off the train, they lined us up in ranks to march to barracks already prepared for us. We sloshed through the muddy countryside, and it took us more than an hour to reach our destination. I didn't have the stamina or the wherewithal to notice what was going on around me, I just walked because they told me to. Thank G-d, I still had Mrs. Gross's coat and the two scarves she had given me.

We walked through a large iron gate to get to the barracks. Inside the camp there were several buildings, each one holding about twenty girls, divided up according to their geographical origins. Most of the girls who had gotten there before me were from Chrzanow, and I knew a few of them.

In this camp, that held about a 1,000 girls, they assigned each of us a bunk made of wooden slats with ticking that was stuffed with hay. In my so-called Green Barrack, we were responsible for keeping our area clean. There was a latrine about fifty feet from the building, but there was no running water.

The camp elder, the *Jüden Altester* (the senior Jewish woman) was Mitzi Mehler, who called us all to an *Appell* in the central part of the camp. At the *Appell* she announced the everyday rules that we needed to obey. She told us we would get up at 5 a.m. for an *Appell*, that we would get six slices of bread a day and a soup for dinner (water with potato peels), that curfew was at 7 p.m. and that we were expected to keep quiet and strictly obey orders.

The next morning we were marched to the Gruschwitz factory, a trip of about forty-five minutes. We were marched in to the large, four-storey high-building, through a single door. Once inside, they immediately directed me to my job on the ground floor where, I discovered, they made huge spools of thread.

The place was huge, noisy, smelly, and wet. There were hundreds of spinning machines that took fibers and spun them onto large spools. I was assigned to the department where they wet the threads with hot water before they were turned onto the spool, part of the process to avoid shrinkage. The largest spools were made on the first floor and were about twelve inches high.

They had dismissed two Frenchmen whose job it had been to place spindle boards at the machines and then to lift the filled boards and put them onto carts for shipping. Now it became my job to do the work of these two men. Each empty board weighed about ten pounds and when fully loaded about twenty-five pounds. My entire day was spent loading and lifting spools. When I was done with that, I then had to label the spools for shipment to various fabric factories, remembering which spools went to which places. Whenever I made an error, the foreman, a rabid anti-Semite who was always angry, would beat me and knock me to the floor. His assistant was a hunchbacked spinster who hated pretty girls and sadistically beat them at every opportunity.

For the first year, the daily food ration was the quarter-inch thin bread with a little watery soup. Over time this was reduced to a weekly rather than daily ration. This necessitated it being all eaten in one day or it being stolen by the other girls. They were nice girls, but they couldn't help themselves. It was the purpose of the Germans to dehumanize us and, very often, they succeeded. They made us break every basic human civility and forced us to lie and steal in order to survive.

With the new food distribution, they would also let us have one boiled potato in its skin (one potato, once a week). Because I had to eat all my bread in one day, I never had the chance to make the potato sandwiches the other girls were able to create. I missed that, but every time I tried to save my bread it would disappear, so I ate it all as soon as I got it. The rest of the week, however, there was no food to be had, unless one found alternative means of acquiring some.

One of the girls who worked in the kitchen wanted me to be her little bootlick. There was a Polish camp word for it, *przydupnik*. She wanted me to scrub her back and do her chores and in return she would give me food. But my parents had raised me with such family pride that I would rather go hungry than lose my dignity.

About six months into my slave labor at the thread factory, I was outside in the gated area around our barracks when I suddenly spotted a familiar face. Out of all the people in the world, I could not believe that there was Maria, the maid who had saved me from the wrath of my parents whenever I hid my sandwich behind the armoire of our old home. She saw me and was shocked. I asked her through the fence how she came to be there, and she told me that she was working as a slave laborer for the Germans, too, but was not kept in a barracks. She told me that she had to report to work every day and lived not far away. I told her that my entire family had been killed. She cried and told me how much she really loved my mother. She had a few sandwiches with her and squeezed them through the bars of the gate so that I would have something to eat. As we parted I was hopeful that my chances for survival in the camp had just improved. But, after that meeting, I never saw Maria again.

• • •

Every day was the same. We would get up at 5 a.m., no matter what the weather, and we had to stand in line for an *Appell*. After the roll call, we lined up for our breakfast — ersatz coffee. Then we were marched to the factory, where we would work all day long. At the end of the day we were marched back to the barracks, again made to stand in line for another *Appell* and then a meal of watery soup. Then we were free to collapse onto our bunks.

Once, one of the girls from our group attempted to escape. She was caught and every one of us, in the typical manner of German collective punishment, had our heads shaved in reprisal. As my long, luxuriant black hair was cut from my head, I cried. It would take almost eighteen months for it to grow back — and then I would soon lose it again.

One day, in the fall of 1944, as we stood once again during an *Appell*, I noticed that a tomato vine growing near our fence had produced a tomato. I had fantasized about these tomatoes and, not thinking, I reached out and picked it. No sooner did I have it in my hand then a *kapo*, Mitzi Mehler's assistant, Rifka, attacked me. I had no idea she was watching that closely, but she had come up behind me and the next thing I knew I was slapped across the face as she screamed at me incoherently. She dragged me to the camp *commandant*, who grabbed a pair of scissors and chopped off my regrown hair right to the scalp. As the now sole bald women in our barracks, I used one of the scarves Mrs. Gross gave me to cover my head. I would later use the other one to barter for a real sandwich from the man who ran the elevators in the factory. It was the most delicious sandwich I ever ate in my life — simple German bread and butter — but I have never eaten anything that tasted that good.

• • •

At the end of 1944, hundreds of women from other countries were brought to our barracks. They had no idea what was in store for them, and at first they refused to eat the food — it repulsed them — or to use the latrines. They soon discovered that it was eat or die, and that they needed to take every opportunity they could to keep themselves clean.

Cleanliness was always an issue. There was one water pump for the whole barracks and the only way we could wash was to collect water in our soup bowls. We would use what we could — no one had soap — and for some strange reason, we didn't, thank G-d, have a lice problem.

In the winter of 1944, as usual, we were very hungry. With the aid of some of my fellow prisoners I decided to raid the cellar underneath our barracks and try to "organize" some potatoes. "Organize" was the term we used for what in another time or another place would have been called stealing. But this wasn't stealing, this was survival. As everything that we ever owned had been taken from us, including our bodies, whatever was necessary to continue to survive was deemed appropriate.

When the SS overseers were asleep, I went down to the cellar, posting one of the other girls as my lookout. There I found a small sack, filled it with potatoes and brought it up to our barracks. In the meantime, a few of the other girls in our group took wooden slats from some of the bunks and fed them into the potbelly iron stove that warmed our building. Creating a blockade around the stove so as to prevent outsiders from witnessing what we were doing, we baked the potatoes and then wolfed them down, enjoying them for the few moments they lasted. Luckily, no one got caught that night. The Nazis would have shot us had they discovered our act.

For some reason, once a month in their special clinic, the

Germans x-rayed our chests to check for cancer or tuberculosis. If anyone had a spot on her lungs, she was immediately deported to Auschwitz. I firmly believe that working in the wet thread factory was for me a blessing, because at the dry thread factory where most of the girls worked they regularly developed lung problems and were sent away. Perhaps the water kept the dust down and saved my lungs — for a time.

• • •

All this time we had no idea what was going on in the real world. Unlike in other camps, we had no access to information at all. In those camps it was possible to figure out what was going on, when it was Shabbos or a Jewish holiday. And even those who did have access to news weren't giving us any information. We were cut off from everyone.

The only entertainment we could provide for ourselves was singing, so we sang Russian songs, Polish songs, and Yiddish songs, like *"Off'n Pripitchik"* and the *"Partisaner Hymn,"* which became very popular in 1943 and spread to the camps like wildfire through the underground. Everyone was singing it.

But our days were long and tedious. Work and hunger was our mainstay, so there was always a temptation to try to escape. One of the girls on our shift again tried but was caught. The girl's punishment was getting her head shaved, and all of us on that shift had to suffer the same fate. Once again, I was bald, but now I had twelve girls with me in the same condition.

My group was an odd lot. Most of us were still wearing the clothes we wore when we first came to the camp two years earlier. On our feet all we had were wooden clogs. Luckily, I still had Shlamek Gross's coat. And now all of us were bald.

One cold, bitter day at the beginning of 1945, they lined us all up for an *Appell*. Usually, they divided us up, putting the Polish girls in one group and the girls from other countries in another. This time, no division was made. Right away I realized that something unusual was about to happen, but I had no idea what it would be. And then they gave us the order to march, our group of Polish girls at the lead.

As snow began to fall, they marched us out of the camp. The road was icy and, with only wooden clogs for traction, many slipped and fell. Some of us helped each other to stay upright. They marched us down the middle of the road, guards on either side. If someone fell, she would be jabbed with a rifle butt and ordered to get up, *"Shnell!"* (quickly). If we didn't move fast enough, they would beat us.

All of us were terrified of being shot. We had no food and no water. Still we marched on — hour after hour, thirsty and hungry, our bellies roiling, our bodies aching. As darkness overwhelmed us, we at last came to a large stable. Huddled into the rank, smelly building, our guards didn't have to order us to collapse onto the floor.

At about six, the weather still bitter cold, the guards woke us and made us continue our hellish march. On and on we marched, our destination unknown, with cold, hunger, and misery our traveling companions.

Days passed, and without food and water many collapsed on the side of the road. Those the Germans did not beat to death for not moving fast enough had already marched to the Next World, dead from starvation. Such was the hunger that some of the women would go through the horse droppings to retrieve any undigested foodstuffs.

About a week into the march my friend Surka Bochner-Mintz began to suffer more and more the ravages of our travel. We had grown up together in Chrzanow and were close. When I saw how tired and hungry she was, I realized that I was not in much better shape and that I needed to do something if we were going to live through this experience.

As we marched along it became obvious that our German captors were in trouble. There were rumors everywhere that the Allies were coming. And the soldiers guarding us weren't as careful as they had been before; some of them even disappeared as we marched along. We also saw German civilians running away. They thought that the oncoming Americans would shoot them on sight and so didn't want to be on the front lines.

Earlier on our march, we had passed a German town that looked abandoned. Milk cans had been turned over on the roads, doors were locked and no one was around. It seems that a group of foreign girls that had left the camp before us had scared all the inhabitants of the towns they passed through. They had acted like wild animals whenever they found something to eat and had destroyed that which they didn't use. By the time we got to these towns, no one wanted to help us.

Through the trees, I saw some houses of a small town and naively decided that I would try to save Surka and myself by going to ask for some food. It was still daylight, but if there was any chance for success I needed to make a move immediately. I made sure none of the Germans were looking and ran out of the line into the woods, hiding behind trees while working my way toward the town. It is impossible to describe how terrified I was, but I felt that if I didn't take the chance we would die from hunger.

G-d was looking after me, and soon I found a two-story house made of brick with a little garden out front. I took a deep breath and knocked on the door. A woman in her mid-thirties answered the door with a smile. Her hair was blonde and tied back in a bun. In German I told her that my parents had fled and that I was left alone — a German orphan; that I needed some food and a place to sleep for the night. Her husband joined her at the door and they both invited me in.

For the first time in years, I felt like a human being. They showed me to a private bedroom and handed me some towels and soap as they led me to the bathroom. I was in seventh heaven. The bathroom was completely modern and had hot- and cold-running water. I had only seen this once before, in my Uncle Itche's apartment in Chrzanow.

With the door securely locked, I washed out my clothing and tried to clean myself up as best I could. The wonder of warm water on a frozen body is one of G-d's miracles. When I came out of the bathroom and went into the kitchen, there was hot food waiting for me — another miracle. I had to use great self-control to keep from throwing myself upon the food and stuffing it into my mouth. Instead, I used the beautiful table manners my parents had taught me.

During the meal my hosts asked me some questions and I was forced to respond to their graciousness with lies; I couldn't let them know that I had escaped from a death march. I went to sleep in a nice, cozy bed and thought how wonderful it would be if I never went back to the march. But there were a number of things that bothered me. I could not abandon Surka and one other friend who was dying of starvation as well, and I looked too Jewish to last in that environment for very long. I decided I would be better off taking some food from these nice people and bringing it back to my friends on the march.

The next morning they fed me and packed a bag with thick

slices of bread and butter. I thanked them, said goodbye and headed back to the road. As I walked along I no longer carried myself like a prisoner and tried to pass as a German. I returned to the area where I had last seen our group but they were nowhere to be found. Not seeing the girls anywhere on the road, I asked several passersby if they had seen a transport of girls under guard. They directed me toward Marienbad.

I walked on for a few hours and, after dark, came upon a stable, sneaked in and found the group of foreign girls from the camp. They were all packed together. Not wanting to catch lice from them after working so hard to clean myself, I spent the night standing against the wall, hanging on to my bag of bread for dear life.

In the morning, we were once more ordered to march and, after several hours, we eventually joined up with my original Polish group. Surka was still with them, so I pulled her to the side and gave her and a few others pieces of my bread.

We were now in the third week of our march. Many had died. And then we came upon Gross-Rosen, one of the Third Reich's major concentration camps. We saw the barbed wire fences and the signs, and were even able to speak to some of the inmates who were near the fence. But we did not stop here; our journey was not yet over.

A few days later we came to Flossenberg. It was a very large death camp for men only. The inmates looked like skeletons, literally, walking dead. They called them *Musselmen*. These were people who no longer cared if they lived or died, they just fulfilled the roles assigned them by the Reich, burying, cremating, sorting the remains of the dead, any filthy thing the Nazis deemed necessary. They were literally the soul-less, waiting for their own call to perdition.

All of us from the Neusalz transport who survived the

march were kept together and ordered to line up for yet another *Appell*. They then took all the rest of our possessions, what little we had. The only valuables I had were my family photos, but they took them all away. Then they marched us to a disinfection/delousing center and had us strip naked. We feared that our time had come, that our lives were now over. But there was no gas in these showers. Instead, they threw powder on us and gave us rags that didn't fit. They gave large people small sizes and small people large sizes, everyone having to exchange whatever clothes they had for the *shmattes* (rags) now being thrown to us. It was very demeaning. But the most amazing thing that happened while we were in that terrible place with men dying all around is that they fed us a decent soup that actually tasted good and seemed to have some nutritional value. They then showed us to barracks with no beds, where we slept on the floor.

The *Appell*s and the feeding routine went on for two days. On the third day, a bitter-cold day that must have been at the end of February, they put us in cattle cars, a hundred people squeezed into a wooden car with no windows, no water, no latrine but a single bucket, no room to do anything but stand. We had no idea where they were going to take us or what they were going to do to us. The stink of these huddled bodies was only minimized by the stink of fear the pervaded our every breath. It was dark, and we were all terrified.

We were on that train for eight days with no food or water or fresh air. Many of the girls died. By the time we got to where we were going, the stench in the car was unbearable. How any of us survived that trip was a miracle, but we didn't know how much worse it was about to get. The only thing that kept us alive was our will to live.

The train finally stopped in Celle, a charming town in

Lower Saxony that dated back to the ninth century. Situated on the banks of the river Aller, Celle has one of the few remaining *shuls* in Germany (built in 1740) that hadn't been destroyed by the Nazis. This was because an important leather factory was located next door, and any attempt to burn down the *shul* would have affected the factory as well.

Celle was the end of the line. From there we had to walk about five miles to a facility whose name we did not even know.

And then came enlightenment. After our long march we were finally welcomed to our new home, Bergen-Belsen.*

The first sight that greeted us was a pile of emaciated naked women's bodies that was about forty-feet square by about eight-feet high. But that horror dwindled next to the size of the camp. It was huge. It was so big you couldn't see from one end to the other. Even the field where they called the *Appell*s was larger than anything I had ever seen before.

Once they assigned us to a primitive hut, about forty by twenty feet, they left us alone. Surka and I stayed together. There was an earthen floor, no stove, no water, no bunks. There was no place to lay your head, and nothing with which to cover yourself. And our job was to just lie there, one body after another — the living and the dead.

It was the beginning of March. The rumors about the Allies advancing continued, but meanwhile there were Germans all around us. For us, though, none of this seemed to matter.* There was no food and no potable water, just

---

* Bergen-Belsen was a National Socialist concentration camp in the Celle district, built between March and mid-July 1943. It was intended for about 10,000 female and male Jewish prisoners of various European nationalities, for whom emigration was promised in exchange for German returnees. At first the inmates were not to be drafted for work; only after 1944 was compulsory labor required of some inmates (unloading railroad cars, excavation work, and so on). Bergen-Belsen was divided into individual sections, the largest of which was the "star camp" (*Sternlager,* named after the "Jewish star").

people dying everywhere — from starvation, from filth, from disease. The only saving grace was that none of us were being called to work in any kind of labor detail, although some form of work, even for the Germans, would have been better than the uselessness we felt. Obviously, the system was breaking down, but we couldn't figure out what would happen next. All we knew at this point was despair. We had come so far, survived for so long, and now it all seemed so hopeless. Bergen-Belsen deadened whatever spirit we had left. I watched one day as a mother and daughter fought

---

Second came the so-called camp for neutrals (*Neutralenlager*), which housed Jews from neutral states who could not be exchanged. Food, housing, and hygienic conditions corresponded to the usual inadequate standards common to concentration camps. The inmates were bullied and mistreated by block and detachment leaders despite the fact that Bergen-Belsen passed for a camp with preferential treatment.

In 1944 there were exchange operations with Palestine (222 persons) for German citizens interned there; with Switzerland (1,685 Hungarian Jews) for a per capita rate of about $1,000; and with the United States and North Africa (about 800 persons) in exchange for German citizens interned in the United States. In the course of 1943, sick inmates from other concentration camps were brought to a separate section (the convalescent camp), which eventually housed about 2,000 inmates. The lack of medicines and the miserable hygienic conditions led to many deaths. In June and July 1944, in particular, many seriously ill inmates were killed with injections of phenol. Besides the "convalescent camp," an "induction camp" (tent camp) was set up in mid-August for Polish women. It was totally overcrowded by late 1944 and early 1945 with thousands of sick female inmates from Auschwitz.. Toward the end of the war Bergen-Belsen served as a collection camp for many thousands of inmates evacuated from other concentration camps. Catastrophe resulted, and after February 1945 new arrivals were not even registered. Losses through hunger, infectious disease, and exhaustion were terrible. From early January to mid-April 1945, some 35,000 people died in Bergen-Belsen. When the commandant, Josef Kramer, handed over the camp to the British on April 15, 1945, Bergen-Belsen still held about 60,000 survivors, of whom 13,000 died of exhaustion and disease after being liberated. Kramer was sentenced to death by the British and executed; his predecessor, Rudolf Haas, was declared dead in 1950.

The Enclopedia of the Third Reich, Christian Zentner and Friedemann Bedurftig, eds. (NY: Da Capo Press, 1997), 78-79.

Women in Bergen-Belsen after liberation

over some margarine that had somehow been distributed to the camp inmates. I remember, I chewed the paper from that margarine for days.

There was nothing to do every day except walk around this huge charnel house of the dead and dying — the ground filthy with waste, bodies everywhere. To alleviate some of the problem, some of the men set up a system to bury the dead. Having dug huge pits, these now served as mass graves.

Surka and I found some friends and thus stayed in a small group. One day, as I walked through the grounds, I couldn't believe my eyes. I thought I recognized someone, but it was hard to tell. I thought it might be my cousin Goldzia Lauber from Jaworzno. I started yelling, "Goldzia, is that you?" and she yelled back with joy, *"Frimciu! Dus bist die?"* In Yiddish she was asking me if I was really me. We weren't recognizable. My hair was still very short and I was thinner than I had ever been.

Goldzia worked for the Germans in the camp's main kitchen. Though she knew I was starving and earnestly wanted to help me, she was afraid to smuggle out any food because the workers there were always closely watched. If caught, the punishment was either a thorough beating or death. Once, however, she was able to bring me a huge turnip. I tried to hide it, but the Germans caught me with it and forced me to kneel on the ground for an entire day. Then, after they let me up, they made me bite into it. It was inedible; hard as a rock.

In the first week of April, after six weeks in this totally dehumanizing environment, the Germans disappeared. Our new guards were Hungarians. On April 14, the Hungarians killed a few women they had pulled from the crowd. It was enough to frighten us terribly.

The next day, we woke up and heard loud clanking noises and big machines. Then we heard voices speaking in English. We ran out of the hut and found British tanks in the camp. Someone announced in English over a microphone, "The war is over! The war is over!"

I don't remember how many tanks or how many soldiers there were. We didn't know enough to express joy or happiness — we still didn't know what was happening to us. The bodies were still everywhere. The Germans wanted to hide what they were doing, but didn't manage to finish the job before the British arrived.

I later learned that the reason they marched us around Europe in those last days was to get us away from the Western front, so they could try to hide what they were doing to the Jews. The more that died on the way, the cheaper it was for the Germans. The crazy part of it was that Hitler, knowing that he was losing the war, was so intent on killing every last Jew that he used all his military options to move Jews toward the death camps to exterminate them. Fanatical madman that he was, he would sooner kill Jews than save his own people.

Now the British had liberated us. Shocked by the huge

number of inmates at the camp, they were totally unprepared for the medical emergency that greeted them. Though they set up rudimentary medical facilities, people continued to drop like flies. In addition to the already prevalent starvation and diseases, typhus had now grabbed the camp as well.

One of the main problems the British encountered was feeding the Bergen-Belsen population. Few had any experience as to how to deal with the victims of starvation. As such, when they gave people foods that were high in fats, people's digestive tracts literally exploded. In fact, 14,000 people who had survived the Holocaust were unable to survive the liberation of Bergen-Belsen.

Toward the end of the first week after the British arrived, I conspired to put to use the English my mother had paid a tutor to teach me. They had pitched a large tent for use as a hospital and, having seen the clean beds in the clinic there, I wanted nothing more than to lie down on those sparkling white sheets. So I approached a British officer and said that I wasn't feeling very well and asked if he could get me admitted to the clinic. Though I believed I wasn't as sick as some of the others, I so dearly wanted to feel the clean whiteness envelop me that I overcame my guilt. Astounded to hear British English, the officer acquiesced to my request.

I had believed that I wasn't sick, but the very next day, while lying in a clinic bed, I suddenly became delirious. I was indeed sick with typhus and hadn't known it. By asking for help when I did, I had saved my own life.

After the delirium I lapsed into a coma for about three weeks. When I woke up, the nurse told me I was lucky, that I was okay and that I needed to leave because they needed the bed. The only problem was that I had no underwear, no shoes and no clothing. All I had was a sheet and a gray blanket.

Another girl in a bed nearby decided to help me out. She created a whole wardrobe for me out of scraps. She made a blouse out of a sheet, and a skirt and suit jacket out of a gray military blanket. I even remember the style. It was a blouson jacket that was belted at the waist. She did it for me out of the kindness of her heart, and I regret that I don't remember her name because she was one of the most decent people I have ever met. I don't remember how I got a pair of shoes either, but someone made them appear. The day I walked out of the clinic was the first time since the day I had that bath in the farm house while on the death march to Bergen-Belsen that I felt like a woman.

• • •

A few days after I came out of the clinic, I was moved to a large building in Celle that used to house German soldiers, probably once a garrison building. Goldzia's brother, Aciek (Aaron) Lauber,* watched over me and made sure I didn't go out with boys. There were one thousand men living in that building and just five girls. Goldzia and I were two of them. If a man would come by to ask us for a date, Aciek would warn him that he would be punished if he laid a hand on me.

Longing for the better times of the past, I joined a group of Bais Yaakov girls that had been

Bais Yaakov girls after liberation

organized by Rebbetzin Esther Wagner in what used to be one of the barracks for the Nazi officers in Bergen-Belsen. We had lessons on Shabbos and other religious matters, though much of our time was spent figuring out how to get our hands on kosher food to eat. There, I soon found my cousin Shmuel Engelberg and many family friends from different parts of Poland living nearby. Later, many other families would live in those buildings and many children would be born there and in the hospital in Celle. Today, the camp is a museum and a NATO base.

Aciek* continued to watch over me, making sure that no man made untoward advances. But soon a man appeared to whom even Aciek gave his seal of approval, the man with whom I would spend the next fifty-three years of my life.

---

*   Aciek eventually married Dyncia Rosenfeld and also moved to the United States. We remain close friends. Goldzia married Moniek Goldstein in Celle.

Chapter 4

Shimon's Story

Bordering the Ukraine to the east and Slovakia to
the south and the Polish regions of Slask to the
west and Mazowsze to the north, the Malopolska
region of Poland is an area of charming beauty.
With medieval towns and castles dotting the hillsides and
the Carpathian Mountains covered with the colors of diverse vegetation, it is a perfect place for those fond of diverse
scenery.

For centuries, the Jews of Poland thrived in this region,
and it became famous as a major center of Jewish culture.
With such towns like Krakow, Przemysl, Jaroslaw, and Lvov,
there arose a Jewish life rich in shuls, schools, and Jewish
institutions of renown. Home to many chassidic sects — in
Bobowa, Brzesko, Dombrowa Gornicza, Dombrowa Tarnowska, Lezajsk, Rzeszow, Stary Sacz, and Nowy Sacz — the
hallmarks of all that was Jewish flourished in this homeland
so far from Eretz Yisroel. In Krakow alone one could find the
Old Synagogue, the Remu Synagogue, the Synagogue of Wolf
Popper, the *Kowea Itim L'Torah* House of Prayer, the High

Synagogue, the Synagogue of Isaac, the Kupa Synagogue, the Tempel Synagogue, B'nei Emuna, Chevra Tehillim, and a host of smaller shuls and *shtieblech* that catered to a population of almost 60,000 Jews. Here, too, were schools: the Hilfstein Hebrew High School, the Cheder Ivri School, the Tachkemoni High School, the Jewish School of Handicrafts, and the Tarbut School — all dedicated to the furtherance of a Jewish life and learning.

Into this community Shimon (Simon) Laufer was born on March 21, 1921, in the Podgórze section of Krakow to a chassidish family that followed the Bobover Rebbe. He lived with his mother, Mindl, his father, Sholem, three sisters and two brothers and a maid, in a two-room apartment. His parents worked together in their grocery store. The children learned Polish in school and spoke mostly Yiddish with their parents. In the summertime, the family would travel by train to Rabka, to the same resort where my family sent me, and would stay for a month. Somehow, during our childhoods, I never met him or his siblings.

As a small boy Shimon attended public school in the morning and went to cheder in the afternoons with his brothers. His sisters attended the local Bais Yaakov. All of them learned to sing songs in Yiddish. On Fridays, the family would visit their paternal grandparents in Krakow, and sometimes they would travel to see his maternal grandparents, who lived next door to us in Chrzanow. In all the years before the war I never met Shimon there, either.

On Shabbos and *yom tov* the men went to shul and, like us, the women stayed home. When they came home from shul, his father would make Kiddush for the family. Their religious observance was very strict. In those days, even at our house, no one was allowed to sit in the father's chair, even on

The Laufer patriarchs, Yankel, Mayer, and Sholem

weekdays. On Shabbos, no one was allowed to visit friends, though most of the family lived in the same apartment house. Shabbos was definitely a family day.

After a Shabbos morning breakfast of cake and coffee, the men would rush off to shul, pick up the *cholent* on the way home, and make Kiddush for a meal of fish, chicken, and *cholent*. After lunch everyone would take a nap, and then the men would go back to shul for *Minchah* and *Ma'ariv*, which also gave the boys a chance to play with their friends for an hour or so.

In 1936, at the age of fifteen, Shimon decided that his future lay in the business world. After working for someone who used boxes to pack hardware, he determined that he could make a ten-groshen profit on such boxes if he became a supplier. Within his first week of business, he was already making between 150 to 200 zlotys a week, whereas most people averaged just 30 zlotys. Within his first year, he quit school and was making more money than his parents made in their grocery business. A dutiful son, every Friday he would hand over almost all of his earnings to his parents.

In time, his father decided that the grocery business was

a failure, and he sold it for what Shimon made in a single week. He then went to work for his son as a business adviser. Following the precept of honoring thy father and thy mother (he had tremendous respect for his parents), Shimon treated his father as if he was the real boss of the business. And his father accepted the title, even sometimes objecting when the workers called his son *Pan* (Mister). "He's too young to be called 'mister,'" he would tell them.

Eventually, Shimon and his father did lots of business with vintners and liquor distillers who needed wooden boxes to ship their glass bottles. The business prospered, and Shimon even hired two men to work for him for a few zlotys a day.

In 1937, one of Shimon's sisters married and moved to

Mindl and Sholem Laufer, Simon's parents

Israel. He would not see her for twenty years.

The business continued to prosper and, in early 1939, Shimon, now a young man with prospects, went on his first official "date" without a chaperone. But then the war broke out.

On September 6, 1939, the Nazis marched into Krakow. On September 21, Reinhard Heydrich, head of the Nazi Security Service (the *Sicherheitsdienst*) ordered the dissolution of all Jewish communities with populations of less than five hundred people. All who did not perish in the forced relocation by his *Einsatzgruppen* were assigned to newly established urban ghettos, where thousands of people were squeezed into cramped quarters usually in the most rundown areas of a city. With little food, unsanitary health conditions, no medicine, and little to do but suffer under the Nazi boot, many perished — which was the Nazis' true goal.

Few Poles came to the aid of their fellow Jewish citizens; in fact, many were all too glad to commandeer the homes and businesses of their former Jewish neighbors. They were also eager to turn in any Jews who might have escaped the Nazi roundup. After the war, the Poles would deny any complicity in German activities, but we survivors know the truth. The Jews who would die in Kielce, Nowy Targ, and other towns in Poland bear testimony to Polish rapaciousness and cruelty. (As with all generalizations, however, there were some exceptions. One of these "righteous gentiles" was Tadeusz Pankiewicz, an apothecary who risked his life to save Jews. Licensed to operate in the Krakow ghetto, this brave pharmacist provided medical assistance and even hid Jews from the Nazi persecutors. In 1983, the Muzeum Pamieci Narodowej would commemorate his heroism.)

During the war, those seeking to save Jews ensnared in the Nazi grip discovered that there was a way to rescue some of their brethren. The Nazis, concerned about the several hundred thousand Germans living in Latin America, feared reprisals if those holding Latin-American documents were treated harshly in Europe. The Nazis thus permitted Jews with Latin-American passports to live outside of ghettos and did not force them to wear armbands. With this information in hand, as well as bribes ranging from 500 to 3,000 Swiss francs, these countries were "persuaded" to issue protective papers to those who could afford to pay for them. Because of his contacts, Shimon was able to obtain such papers from Argentina, papers that also enabled him to stay in business.

Somehow, Shimon ended up selling kosher wine to the Nazis. Though his former customers' businesses had been Aryanized, the *Troyhandlers* continued to do business with him.

Eventually, his family was forced to move to Wieliczka, a small town famous for its salt mines, eight miles from Krakow. They took over an apartment and moved some their things by horse and wagon. By then, Shimon no longer had access to barrels of wine, and he went into the black market, where he dealt in gold and jewelry.

The Laufer family:
(l-r) Mindl, Israel, Miriam, Chemie, Hanka, Sholem, Shimon, and Rachel

In December 1940, Nazi terror began in earnest. Jewish property was seized, synagogues were burned, and thousands of Jews were forced from their homes.

Soon the Nazis liquidated the ghetto in Wieliczka and deported everyone to Bochnia. There, Shimon lived in an apartment next door to his beloved Rebbe, Rabbi Shlomo Halberstam, the Bobover Rebbe. Simon used to say that the Rebbe's influence strengthened him in his resolve to resist the Nazis.

"The Rebbe's words gave me the strength and the vigor to bear the trials, pain, troubles, and persecution of the murderers, may their name be accursed," he once told Gershon Jacobson of the *Algemeiner Journal*, a Yiddish newspaper published in New York City.

Operating on the black market was, of course, fraught with danger. When the Nazis caught Simon's brother with forbidden goods, they killed him. His parents, separately, went into hiding, but then Shimon and his father were discovered and taken to a camp near Krakow called Plaszow. The last time Shimon saw his father was when the Nazis put him on a bus for an overnight trip. His destination: Auschwitz.

In the morning, Shimon escaped and went back to Bochnia, where he found his mother. He still had his Argentinian protective papers, and he commuted to Krakow daily to do "business" under an assumed name.

On March 3, 1941, the Krakower *Zeitung* announced that all Jews living in Krakow must relocate to the *Judisher Wohnbezirk*. The Krakower ghetto had now become a reality. From March 3rd to the 20th, 18,000 people were squeezed into 320 buildings in the Lubelsk region, into an area with dimensions of 656 x 437 yards. Without the necessities of life, famine and disease quickly began to take their toll.

On the last day he was in Bochnia, Shimon approached a Polish man who owed his brother 32,000 zlotys. His brother had sold gold bullion to this fellow and Shimon went to collect the payment due. When they met, the man asked him to wait, went into a store to use a telephone, came out and asked Shimon to meet his wife a few blocks away. This whole business made Shimon very uncomfortable; he was afraid and felt that something was crooked about the deal. He realized that he shouldn't go to meet the wife, but it was too late. The man had turned him into the Germans and the SS was waiting for him. Shimon was arrested on suspicion of being a Russian spy; in reality, the man had turned him in for being a Jew. Shimon, now in SS custody, found himself on the way to the infamous Montelupich Prison.

After Shimon was fingerprinted, the SS put him in chains and brought him to the Jewish police station in the Krakow Ghetto, where he stayed for a number of weeks until the ghetto was liquidated. Afterward, they took forty to fifty prisoners from the jail on a two-and-a-half hour bus ride to Auschwitz. On the bus ride people began jumping off in an attempt to escape. Shimon contemplated taking a chance, but when he saw how good the marksmen were who were guarding the transport and how all of those who jumped were shot, he decided to stay on the bus.

One of the people Shimon left behind in Bochnia was a longtime associate with whom he had been friendly for many years. Before the war he had been a man of impeccable character, a responsible person whom many considered a confidante. But unbeknownst to his friends, the war had changed him. Using his influence and connections, he became a power broker and he developed contacts with the Germans in order to ply his trade.

239.	Breufeld Isak	ledig	10.11.	Skaleosna J	E.B.	
240.	Urbaoh Aron	verh.	19.3.886	Stara Olsza Kąt 3.	E.K.	
241.	Lasenga Ssulim	"	7.2.910	Krasiokiego 9	8567/4	
242.	Sohneeweis Jakób	"	18.4.896	Dąbrowskiego 16	5528	
243.	Niedermann Mojzess	"	1885	Pl.Nowy 9	E.K.	
244.	Wagner Icek	"	15.12.906	Jakóba 31	E.K.	
245.	Efaktor Jakób	led.	9.12.901	Nowy Korosyn	E.K.	
246.	Sohanter Chaim	"	10.9.924	Chrsanów-Jagiellonki 2.	E.!	
247.	Feiweles Jakób	verh.	23.5.904	Bronowice 4	E.K.	
248.	Urbaoh Leopold	led.	27.2.924	Prąd.Czerw. 3	E.K.	
249.	Laufer Szxmon	"	21.3.921	Rynek Podg.3.	E.K.	
250.	Trimaman Wolf	verh.	12.12.886	Dajwór 53	E.Z.	
251.	Kornfeld Chiel	verh.	1884	Długa 55	E.K.	
252.	Mendlowics Mendel	"	25.3.876	Rękawka 33	2956	
253.	Hárschprung Simon	"	24.6.888	Sebastiana 16	348,691	
254.	Kluger Salomon	"	23.6. 882	Szewska 17	E.K.	
255.	Schaffer Aron	"	1895	Kołłątaja 8	E.K.	
256.	Friedenberg Josef	"	17.2.887	Prokocim	E.K.	

ad N.228 siehe Transportliste Nr.5/42 - Dębica 14/XII,1940.

In 2007, on a return to Krakow, I found the German transport document that listed Simon's name (number 249) in the Apothecary museum.

Before his deportation, Shimon had managed to contact this friend and asked him to deliver a message to his mother. With his father gone, Shimon hoped that he could at least provide for his mother through the good graces of his friend. To accomplish this, he gave his friend a diamond ring and asked him to get the ring to his mother, so that if he wasn't around to take care of her, the ring would at least provide her with some money. Shimon asked him not to tell his mother that he was being deported to Auschwitz, and to tell her instead that he was going to smuggle himself over the Hungarian border. He also told him that if he couldn't get the ring to his mother, he should deliver it to the Bobover Rebbe. Needless to say, with Shimon out of the way, the ring was not delivered to anyone. Cruelly, the man also told Shimon's mother of her son's deportation to Auschwitz. To his dying day, Shimon never forgave the man for this betrayal.

Upon his arrival in Auschwitz, there was an initial *selektion,* where he and those with him were processed (identified by the Nazi's meticulous bookkeepers and assigned to camp duties). Shimon watched as a man was shot for going to the right (hard labor) instead of the left (gas chambers). Then, those on the right were sent to the showers, where Shimon described the water as being "not too cold." The men were "disinfected" and had their heads shaved. They were issued striped uniforms and held for a few days.

In Auschwitz, Shimon was fortunate to find two friends he'd grown up with in Krakow, the Obstfeld brothers. They had been assigned to the same barracks, one that held 200 men in bunks that were three tiers high.

Though the Nazis would distribute bread and soup, the rations were so meager that people slowly starved to death. Getting hold of food and water meant life, and so people would do anything to get some — lie, cheat, steal...and sometimes even act like caring human beings.

In the meantime, in the world outside the camp, those Jews who had not already died were now facing the liquidation of the Krakow ghetto. In March 1943, 2,000 of the ghetto's surviving Jews were sent to Plaszow and 2,300 to Auschwitz. Tadeusz Pankiewicz, the pharmacist, witnessed people running on rooftops, hiding in cellars, walking around like lunatics. He was helpful to the Jews at the risk of his life, but he could only watch as old people walked toward the deportation area with religious books in their hands, and as children walked hand-in-hand under the cold eyes of the SS and the *sonderkommandos*. Shots rang out continually, from morning till night, and then there was a stillness. The streets were empty, the pitiful ghetto homes were deserted. From every corridor a cemetery emptiness was felt — the ghetto was no more.

There was a day in 1943 when Shimon and the Obstfelds desperately thirsted for water. Finding a German guard,

Simon persuaded him to give his friends a glass of water in exchange for a pair of boots. One of the brothers, Avrum, took the boots off his feet and gave them to the SS man. In payment, the Obtsfelds gave Shimon a swallow of their water. Until his dying day, Shimon believed that the single gulp of water he received saved his life because it reenergized him. It would keep him going for the next two years of hard labor and imminent death.

• • •

In the winter, Shimon and his group were taken from Auschwitz to Buchenwald by cattle car — with a hundred people jammed into each car without food or water and just one bucket for human waste. Shimon remembers the trip taking three or four hours. When they got to Buchenwald they were tattooed with numbers. For some reason, instead of being recorded as Laufer, Shimon's name was recorded in the Nazi rolls as Wolfeiler. He and his fellow inmates were then assigned the job of piling up dead bodies — thousands of them. When they weren't doing that, they stood around watching people die of starvation or being shot by Nazis.

About ten days after they arrived in Buchenwald, Shimon's group was taken by bus to Jawiszowice, five or six miles away, where they worked in the local coal mines. There they discovered that they were working with Polish people who were brought in from the outside. Some of these people would be stirred enough by pity to offer the starving Jews some food or things they could use. But soon the Germans realized that people were smuggling things back into the camp and began searching the prisoners as a matter of routine.

One time, Shimon was caught trying to steal a blanket into the camp. When the Nazis searched him, they found it under his uniform. Somehow, he had the chutzpah to ask the guards not to do anything to him and to please just leave him alone. But of course they didn't. They pulled him and others caught smuggling that day off to the side and took their names. They were ordered to show up at one of the Nazi offices on the following Sunday. There, each man had to take forty-five lashes across his chest. While Shimon was taking his beating, the German *kapo* who wielded the whip made Shimon count each lash. Shimon lost count, so they started from the beginning and made him count again.

A few weeks later, during an *Appell*, the Germans offered a reward for the names of people who should be reported. Shimon was the only one to raise his hand. He gave them the name of the Polish man who had turned him in years before. He told the Nazis that he'd sold the man 20 or 30 bars of gold. A month after that, in the middle of the night, someone yelled Shimon's name in the barrack. He woke up, terrified. But this time, the Nazis weren't looking to punish him. They informed him that his reward was sausage and 200 loaves of bread. He was given the option of taking his reward as a lump sum or having it rationed. He wisely chose rationing. Many people were jealous, because food meant life, but Shimon knew how to handle it. He was kind and he was smart. During soup distribution in the camps and at the coal mine he would share his portion with others or barter it for needed items.

There was a day when Shimon got sick and was sent to the infirmary, where they put him next to a man who had just died. Shimon held on to his hand, as if he were still alive, and managed to get an extra food ration that was issued to the "body." He found ways to fake being sick and stayed in the infirmary for as long as he could.

For two years, Shimon managed to survive the horrors of Auschwitz, and then, in March 1945, he was sent back to Buchenwald — on a death march. Luckily, Shimon had a pair of shoes and had somehow fashioned a backpack for himself. They walked all day under German guard, and heard people speaking other languages, including English. There were rumors that the Americans were coming, but that didn't mean much to Shimon, because he knew nothing about America at that time. He just kept marching until one day he'd had enough and ran from the line to a nearby house, where he hid in a cellar. There, he found a jacket and some slippers and put them on.

He sat in that place for a few hours as the march continued without him. But then the lady of the house came down to the cellar for some coal and found him. She demanded to know what he was doing there. He didn't know what to do, so he ran out of the house and back to the road, but everyone was gone. A few minutes later he saw a Polish man who wore prisoner clothing working nearby. Shimon told him that he'd just escaped from the march and didn't know what to do. The man advised Shimon to hide in a nearby bunkhouse and wait there and he would bring him some food. He also told Shimon to be patient — the Americans would be arriving in a day or two.

Shimon spent the night in the bunkhouse, and when he woke up that morning he discovered that indeed the Americans were already there. When he saw German soldiers running for their lives, he went into a German apartment and told the woman there that he had escaped from a concentration camp. When she asked him what he wanted to eat, he asked for french fries. They spent hours talking and then it was time to get some sleep. She gave him a bed, but he woke up hungry in the middle of the night and ate two jars of fruit that he found in the kitchen. In the morning, he began vomiting. The woman took him to a hospital, where they discovered that he weighed just 60 kilos (132 pounds).

Shimon did not remember much about those first days in the hospital, because he had typhus and was unconscious most of the time. He was kept clean and fed regularly, and when he finally awoke the nurses and doctors, told him that he had a friend there who was also a patient, another survivor. Shimon went to find him, and though he didn't know the man he introduced himself. The man was incapable of feeding himself, and so Shimon helped the man by feeding him.

Once Shimon knew the war was really over, he began looking for family members who might have survived. He knew one sister was living in Israel and then he heard that his uncle, Berl Laufer, was in Bergen-Belsen, a former concentration camp that had now been turned into a Displaced Person's camp. Uncle Berl worked there with the Central Committee of the survivors that was headed by a certain Yosele Rosensaft. And so, still dressed in his concentration camp uniform, Shimon arrived in Celle and found his uncle in the nearby camp.

It wasn't long before Shimon took notice of me. I told him I was from Chrzanow and that I was the only

Shimon (fifth from the left) at a Bergen-Belsen cemetery, November, 1946

survivor from my family. Though I hadn't known him at the time, Berl Laufer had lived next door to us on Rynek 7 Street. He told Shimon not to let me go because I came from a prestigious family he knew well. He then vouched for me and said it would be an appropriate match.

When Shimon asked me to marry him, I said no. I told him, "Go get yourself a pretty girl. I'm sick and I don't know how to cook. I have a spot on my lung. I'm really not ready to get married."

He said, "You're going to say yes." He told me that his uncle had said not to let me go. Shimon told me, "In honor of that you're going to say yes, you're going to get well. And you will be my wife; you will be my queen."

My cousin Aciek was in favor of the match, though I was still reluctant. I didn't feel I was ready for marriage. Moreover, I didn't think I should impose myself on Shimon. I was still recuperating from typhus, and I also feared that I had contracted tuberculosis and had a spot on my lungs. With all of these *tsuris* (troubles), I didn't want to be a drain on such a good man. Naively, I also still had my dreams of marrying into a higher class of social circumstance. It had been my lifelong goal to marry a rabbi or a doctor, a professional man.

After Shimon proposed, Aciek said that my fantasies of landing a medical doctor or a learned rabbi were just that, fantasies, and that I should wake up and see that this man who was asking me to be his wife was a wonderful man who would take good care of me.

In the meantime, people who knew Shimon were shocked to find that after Montelupich, Auschwitz, and Buchenwald he was still alive. Many girls wanted to marry him, but Shimon only paid attention to me. Noticing how frail I was, he decided that if he wasn't a doctor at least he was going to doctor me.

Berl Laufer (center) at a gathering in Bergen-Belsen, late 1945

Since I was constantly coughing and running a temperature, Shimon started bringing me food. Soon I had on my menu butter, sugar, eggs, and other foods he got from his uncle from the Central Committee of the Bergen-Belsen Survivors. And every few days he would put me on a scale. We were both convinced I had tuberculosis, but I was determined to get better. He would constantly tell me that if I married him he would be my mother, father, sister, and brother all rolled into one, that he would always care for me and make sure I would get well.

In addition to being my doctor, Shimon also decided to become my couturier. Since the Central Committee had a supply of used men's suits, Simon one day asked his uncle if he could get two suits for me and one for himself. Because of the urgent need for suits for all the DP's, his uncle could only let us have one suit apiece. Nevertheless, Shimon gave my suit to a tailor and had it turned into a smartly-tailored women's suit.

Shimon kept showering me with gifts and attention. Was love growing for him? Since he was the first boy I had ever dated, I didn't know if I loved him or not. I thought he was unusually good-natured, and a man that was smart and who knew how to handle himself in any situation...financially and otherwise. I remembered wishing that I had known him during the war, because it was clear he was extremely resourceful and I never would have gone hungry if he had been with me.

Over the next few weeks we went for walks and found out more about each other. We talked about our lives, the war, our parents, our siblings. Shimon grew to love me more and more. One time, when he came to visit, I wasn't home because I had gone to see someone from Chrzanow who had just arrived in Celle. I found out later that Shimon was so sick with worry, jealousy, and anxiety that he actually ran a fever that day.

When I heard about his condition, I went to see him and discovered he was indeed running a fever. He asked me where I had gone and I told him I had gone to see some old friends from my hometown. He was very relieved and, amazingly, the fever quickly abated.

I think it's im-

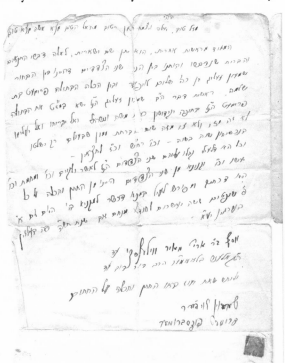

Announcement of our engagement, August 1945

portant to understand how religiously observant we were during the war. Under the Nazis, we ate whatever we were given and worked whenever we were told to work. There was no such thing as Shabbos and *yom tov*, and sometimes those days were marked by the Germans with new tortures, pogroms, extra killings, and extra work. Once we were liberated, however, those of us who came from Orthodox homes tried again to be observant.

As soon as we were liberated, we began keeping Shabbos and tried to make sure that everything we ate was kosher. In those days there were no kosher supervision services or kosher supermarkets. You trusted your local Jewish butcher or you didn't eat meat. If you wanted kosher chicken, you bought a live one and then brought it to someone you could trust to kill it correctly, a *shochet* with a good reputation. Then you had to clean it, soak it and salt it yourself.

It took Shimon about a month to convince me to marry him. Initially, I was reticent; I was a young girl still in shock from the effects of the war. What did I know from men? Was I truly ready to marry? But the more Shimon and I spent time together, the more I realized that I would never find anyone who cared more about me than he did. He was truly a wonderful man. And so, in the middle of July 1945, we began making plans for a wedding.

We went looking for a place to live and found a small apartment in Celle, Zellnerstrasse 29, on the main street. Aciek and Goldzia promised to do all the cooking for the wedding. Simon, by then, had started earning money on the black market and went to Hamburg, where they had a real *shochet*, to order meat for the wedding. I borrowed a gown and veil from a local German woman by giving her cigarettes. More than 300 Bais Yaakov girls who were in Celle came to our

*Friends Rose and Shmuel Engelberg with Shimon and Fran
at their engagement, 1946*

wedding, and one of the girls lent me a pair of white gloves. The girls also gave us a wedding gift of a little silver fork. On October 15, the first wedding since the liberation of Bergen-Belsen took place. The rabbi from the Celle synagogue, Rabbi Israel Moshe Olewski, was our *mesader kiddushin*. Uncle Berl Laufer also attended.

As we stood under the chupah, Shimon asked me, "Should we go on and be religious? Can we go on and be religious after this? After all, look at what has happened to us."

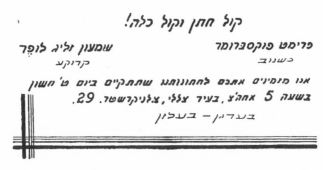

Copy of original wedding invitation for Fran and Simon Laufer, Bergen-Belsen 1945

Wedding invitation, October 16, 1945.

I told Shimon that we had to be Torah observant, religious Jews. I believed that my mother and my father, had they lived, would have wished that we follow in the same footsteps as our parents and grandparents. Though during the war we'd had to do many things to survive, our ultimate survival would have to be in the embrace of observant Judaism. And thus our sacred covenant to each other — and to G-d — was made.

Chapter 5

America

After the wedding, we lived in our apartment in Celle. The landlord was a liquor dealer named Herr Boehner, who would offer Shimon and me samples all the time. My cousin Goldzia taught me how to cook and how to prepare everything according to halachah. This would come in useful as Celle was a main thoroughfare for the *she'aris hapleitah* (Holocaust survivors) looking for their families and relatives. During our time there, we hosted many people as they sought to reclaim some semblance of their lives.

At about this time I found out about my cousin, Chaim Fuchsbrumer-Farber, who had been an officer in the Polish army. After liberation he was one of those who captured the *commandant* of the Majdanek concentration camp. From all my family, he would be the only one to have direct vengeance on the Nazis who so deci-

Chaim Fuchsbrumer-Farber (third from left) after capture of SS officer Hoffman from Majdanek

mated the Jewish people. He participated in his hanging.

• • •

My physical status as a woman was restored exactly one month to the day of our wedding. I was able to enter our marriage with at least the potential to rebuild the Jewish people with my husband. Penniless as I was, I brought with me a precious and generous dowry, the blessing that my parents had conferred upon me: "May you be blessed with children and grandchildren and experience peace with all of Israel." During our time in the camps neither Simon nor I would have dreamed that such a *berachah* could ever be possible — that we could marry, have children, grandchildren, and even great-grandchildren. But we had survived the Holocaust. Our voices had said yes to life, and now life was coming back to us with open arms.

Eventually, we decided that we could not remain in Celle. Though it was a beautiful little town, essentially unaffected by the war, it was not the place to establish roots and begin

Shimon (far left, seated) and Fran (3rd from left, seated), attending the wedding of Goldzia and Moniek Goldstein at Bergen-Belsen

our life together. Too much Jewish blood had been shed on German soil, and we could not see ourselves staying in Germany any longer.

We met a Jewish chaplain who wanted to help us. He asked us where we wanted to live and gave us choices: Sweden, Israel, or America. When Shimon indicated America, the chaplain responded, "Do you have any relatives there?" Shimon explained that his cousins, Regina and Stephen Klein, lived in Brooklyn, New York. (Shimon's Aunt Balka had been married to Simcha Klein, Stephen's father.)

Stephen Klein, head of the Barton's Candy Company in Brooklyn, was a very influential member of the Va'ad Hatzalah, the Orthodox organization that was deeply involved in the rescue of Torah-observant Jews in post-war Europe. Klein agreed to be our sponsor, and he even came to Germany and helped arrange for our papers. But if we ever expected to leave Germany, we had to get to the American zone.

In those days, anything could be bought for coffee, cigarettes, or liquor. With an exchange of some coffee beans that
Shimon was able to acquire on the black market, we were
able to bribe our way out of the British zone and were soon
on our way to Friedberg-Hessen, just a few kilometers from
Frankfurt-am-Main, in the American zone.

• • •

1947 was not an easy year. Since quotas for Poles had already
been filled, it was arranged that we emigrate under the German quota, something that would come back to haunt me.
(Because we had applied for immigration as German citizens,
the Germans were adamant that no future reparations were
to be permitted, hence reparations, *wiedergutmachung gelt*,
were denied me even though I had worked as a slave laborer.)
But we had to leave Germany. The ashes of my dear parents,
siblings, aunts, and uncles surrounded me at every turn, literally driving me out of my mind. Everywhere I turned their
ghosts haunted me; the accursed German soil was a constant
reminder of all that had happened to me and what was once
my family. But we had to wait for the papers that would say
my lungs were clear, that I was not tubercular, so that we could
enter the *goldeneh medina* called America.

And then came that magical day. Our names were called —
we were going to America! We boarded the *S.S. Ernie Pyle*,
a 522-foot converted C4 troop carrier, on March 10, 1947.
Though we had visions of an idyllic trip to a land of family
and rebirth, as with any birth, our emergence into the New
World was not to be an easy one.

The *Ernie Pyle*, having been used as a troop carrier during
the war, was not exactly designed for the comfort of its pas-
sengers. With minimal stabilizers, the ship had a penchant

The S.S. Ernie Pyle

of rolling with the waves, making the stomachs of those on board roll, if not roil, with each rise and fall of the ship's bow. Adding to our discomfiture was the fact that men and women — including husbands and wives — were kept separate.

Because of its cramped quarters and the terrible smell of retching, I spent most of my time above deck. Though food was amply supplied, our stomachs were in constant turmoil and our appetites limited. One day, Shimon brought me an orange, but I became so nauseous that it would be twenty years before I would ever touch an orange again.

In addition to the normal hardships of our ocean crossing, we had the misfortune of encountering a bad storm. Already on a roller-coaster ride before the storm, our situation now became even more perilous. The ship heaved up and down, up and down in the giant waves that threatened to engulf us, and we were forced to wear safety belts as we moved about.

Though the captain tried, eventually he had to concede that it looked unlikely that the *Ernie Pyle* would successfully complete the journey. As water cascaded over the ship he announced that we would have to divert to Plymouth, England, where a replacement vessel would take us the rest of the way to America. Seven days later, the *Marine Flasher* arrived.

All told, it took us about a month to get to the United States. We arrived on April 1, 1947, two days before Pesach.

After we docked, we were met by Isaac Klein, Stephen's younger brother. In his new black Cadillac he took us to the home of Regina and Stephen Klein on Maple Street in Crown Heights, where we spent the first days of Pesach in a beautiful and elegant atmosphere. Such was our welcome to America. On *chol hamo'ed*, Isaac took us to an apartment on Blake Avenue in the Brownsville section of Brooklyn. There, over a fish store, he had found us a room in a small apartment that a woman was willing to rent for $10 a month. The room was a real comedown from the splendor we had just experienced. The apartment was so small that its bathtub was in the kitchen.

(Over the years, Simon and Isaac, both about the same age, became very close. Simon always considered the Kleins like cousins. In addition, Simon was always very appreciative of what the Kleins did for us. In fact, Isaac commented on how of all the people the Kleins sponsored none were as appreciative as Simon.)

Penniless and alone, there were still the remaining days of Pesach to deal with. Though we needed money, Simon was too proud to ask for assistance. After the war Simon had managed to make some money on the black market and had bought himself a fine Omega watch. Now in America, without any money, he pawned our only asset so we could buy some fish,

Simon with Stephen Klein, 1950s

meat, and three pots for the second days of the holiday. We also invited Isaac Klein for *chol hamo'ed* dinner.

Simon recalled, "I went to pawn my watch, saying that we needed money for food for the holiday. I asked for $10 but he said he could only give me $5. I had to make *yom tov* for $5."

Right after Pesach, Simon went looking for a job. With no English and no experience that he could turn into viable employ, Simon could only find work as a cleaner in the 34th Street Barton factory not far from where we lived. But Simon was not to be deterred. He had told me on the ship that he would never work long for anyone, that he would soon be out on his own. And he was true to his word. Even as a cleaner Simon started engaging in entrepreneurial endeavors. He began by peddling nylons after work and selling eggs to his fellow employees. Any way Simon could make an extra dollar, he did so.

In the meantime, I found a job working in Barton's chocolate store on Church Avenue. After work I attended night school. Since I already had some experience with English, my schooling went well and was helpful in my work. But in May 1948 I had to give up my job. Our daughter, Zlate Mindel (Lottie), named after both Simon's and my mother, was born May 8.

Our third-floor walkup —

Simon a U.S. citizen, 1953

Fran and Simon on the Lower East Side, 1950s

now on Powell Street in Brownsville — became even more crowded. We longed for a larger apartment, but what with our rent and now the baby to take care of, money was an all-pressing issue.

Fortunately, during the summer of 1949, we arranged with another family to rent a bungalow in Woodridge, in the Catskills. As everyone knows, New York in the summertime can be very hot. With the new baby and now pregnant with another, it was wonderful to get away from the steamy streets of the city to the clean air and *gemütlichkeit* so many "greeners" enjoyed in the Jewish Alps in the early years after the war.

While Lottie and I were away, Simon gave up our apartment on Powell Street, selling off our furniture as well. Since Lottie and I had a place to stay until Labor Day, Simon figured he could save the rent money for the few months and invest it in his business in an attempt to improve our lot.

At this point in our lives, Simon had stopped working at the factory and had gone into the wholesale hosiery business. Each day Simon would go from house to house selling to the residents, and from business to business selling hosiery to the employees. He was industrious and things started to look up for us.

Giving up our apartment was very scary. Not for Simon,

Lottie and Fran, 1949

though. He always had a confidence that he could over-come any situation. "*Zorg sich nicht, mein kind*" (Don't worry, my child) he said to me. "I will find us something." All the while I had visions of having nowhere to live when the baby and I came home from the country — especially in my condition.

While we were away, Simon saw an ad in a newspaper for a three-bedroom apartment on Greene Avenue, but the ad was very specific in wanting only a doctor for a tenant. Simon called the landlord, a Mr. Lipschitz, posing as Dr. Laufer. Somehow, he managed to convince Lipschitz to rent us the apartment. We had enough time to refurbish and furnish the apartment before Suzie (Shulamit Ruchel, named after my father, Shlome) was born on November 20.

Our new apartment overlooked a park and also had a nearby shul. We began to make friends with our neighbors, especially the Braunfelds and the Obstfelds, and enjoyed our adorable children. Still, I felt an emptiness because I had no family with whom to share my joy.

In 1949, Simon opened a small retail store on Delancey Street in Manhattan with a partner, a man by the name of Ashkenazi. One day, after Ashkenazi had returned after going out for a few hours, he had the temerity to ask Simon about the whereabouts of some inventory missing from a shelf. To Simon, Ashkenazi's question was more than a simply query, it was a slap in the face — tantamount to an accusation of wrongdoing. Then and there Simon ended the partnership. A man of great integrity, he was not about to accept this behavior from anyone.

Simon then opened a wholesale store on Ludlow Street. Because of his energy and drive, the business prospered. But Simon worked long hours and often I was left alone with no one but the children. Already an orphan, I now felt even more lost and alone. Though I loved my two babies dearly, the days were long, the diversions limited, and my days were enveloped in a cloud of despair. I felt more and more helpless, and I was unable to afford a babysitter to get some reprieve. This was further compounded when I became ill and the children had to be taken care of by a social agency. Until I could get back on my feet again I did not even have the children to assuage my pain and my loss.

I had received a letter from my cousin who lived in Tel Aviv, Lotka Goldberg, but had never responded. I now took pen to paper.

Dear Cousin Lotka,

Words cannot express how sorry I am that I did not write to you sooner, especially after the beautiful letter you wrote to us. Your poetic expressions of love and longing truly touched me and Simon deeply. To get to know you better you opened up your heart and revealed on the paper your tragic past and your happy marriage to your dear Isaack. Oh, how I hope and pray to meet you in person someday.

My dear Lotka, let me explain my silence. It has been said that life in America is simplified and supposedly much easier.

Simon and I work hard to build ourselves up, but we still cannot afford to pay for help. I have not a moment for myself to sit down and write. We have two adorable children, Lottie, two years old, and Suzie, a half year old. I am mostly exhausted not only physically but also psychologically. My dear husband is good and stands by me, but our wounds cannot heal — especially when we have nobody close or dear with whom to share our sorrow or joy. Our baby's progress — sitting up, standing up, walking, her first tooth — you feel an everlasting emptiness. Mama, Daddy, where are you when we need you? We live in a neighborhood where I am the only young orphaned mother. I feel different from the others who have that unique treasure — parents, brothers, sisters, aunts and uncles, someone to take over so as not to be enslaved day and night. Not so for us.

Last month I got sick and we were forced to give our children to a nonprofit institute. I could not handle them. I feel better now; the children are home again.

Enough of my crying. I know that you understand now why I could not write to you sooner.

With all out love,
Fran and Simon

P.S. Today is my baby Lottie's second birthday. Happy birthday.

• • •

As the family economic situation grew better in 1950, Simon began to have thoughts of his previous life and family. It had been December 1936 since he had last seen his sister, and so he decided to go to Israel for a visit.

Travel to Israel was by no means a simple trip in those days. It was a long, drawn-out affair and very expensive. Because we were not able to afford tickets for the whole family, and traveling such a long distance with infants would have been very difficult, it was decided that he go alone.

Since he had been in America, Simon's communication with his sister had been sporadic at best, but he did receive an occasional letter from her. With a return address in hand, he was able to locate her building, but she wasn't home. He asked around the neighborhood and discovered that she had taken work as a maid. Simon went to where she worked, not far from where she lived. He knocked on the door and told the owner that he had just come from America and was looking for his sister. Upon entering the house, he saw her there on her knees, cleaning a floor. Frightfully poor, her husband unable to earn enough money for a better lifestyle, his sister had taken on jobs as a house cleaner in order to support her family.

Simon was heartstruck. After she finished her work and they walked back to her apartment, he asked her how much she made doing *sponja*. She said she made $20 a month. He then told her, "From now on you work no more. I'll send you $50 a month." He continued to support his sister for the rest of her life. As time went on, Simon increased the money he sent to his sister, and whenever we or some friends went to Israel, additional sums of money were brought as well. In addition, he decided to help her move out of her one-room apartment and find her a new place to live.

A year later, after having had another successful season in business, Simon and I went to Israel to find her that place. We bought a nice apartment in Cholon (situated in the south of Gush Dan, south to Tel Aviv and east of Bat-Yam) for $5,000 and gave it to her to live in.

In 1967, just after the Six-Day War, we once again went

to Israel and this time found an apartment for ourselves. Wysotzki 18 was a lovely place in Tel Aviv that became our Eretz Yisrael-getaway when we traveled twice a year to the Holy Land.

Having acquired some exquisite, antique Oriental rugs on one of my business trips, I decided to place them in the apartment. I decorated the six-room apartment with custom-made beautiful furniture that was shipped from Italy, put down marble floors and French bathrooms. Because it was difficult to get trained help in Israel, I arranged for the manufacturer himself to do the furniture installation. We then arranged for my cousin Lotka to look after the apartment. She would have a cleaning service come in monthly to make sure it was kept in good condition.

In 1985 Lotka called me in New York with bad news: Our apartment had been burgled. All of my antique rugs had been stolen and our beautiful furniture destroyed. When I arrived in Tel Aviv shortly after, I was heartbroken by what I saw. Our beautiful Italian furniture had been smashed, the rugs gone. All of the work I had done to make our home a place of beauty was now defiled. I decided that I could no longer live in the apartment and immediately put it up for sale.

Chapter 6

Hillcrest

As the business continued to prosper in Simon's capable hands, newcomers to America would find Simon and ask him for work. They would literally stand in line begging for something to do so they could afford to feed themselves and their families. Simon always did whatever he could for them — finding jobs for them in his company sorting hosiery, packaging, and shipping.

When Simon hired Joseph, he found a smart, hard-working and honest individual with whom he could work closely. Joseph's wife, Lea, was my savior as well. Because of Lea, I was able to work in the office part-time while she took care of the children. Life seemed to be getting better — but man plans and G-d laughs.

Sometime earlier, a cousin in Canada had suggested an export venture. This, too, became a successful enterprise. But upon a trip to Europe to collect on a recent shipment, Simon discovered that his cousin had walked off with the invoiced $25,000. Of course their relationship immediately ended, but Simon was now penniless. And of course Simon wouldn't sue because the man was a cousin. "He has a wife and children. G-d will help me and we'll make it again," Simon assured me. But all of our money had been reinvested in the business and now we were broke.

Since Simon had built up a good reputation with his suppliers, he managed to get a $5,000 loan to start a new business. And so, on the corner of Essex and Rivington Streets in Manhattan, the Laufer Department Store was born. (Years later, when the man who had given us the loan himself went bust, Simon would send him money every month to support him. This was the nature of my Simon.)

But there would be another birth that would not be as fortuitous. I had become pregnant again, and being new to Boro Park I had asked the local grocery woman to recommend a doctor for me. Unfortunately, the doctor had little in the way of a compassionate and concerned bedside manner. When I told him I couldn't feel the baby, he disregarded my concerns. *Erev Yom Kippur*, in the eight month of my pregnancy, I was rushed to the hospital; the baby was stillborn. For so long I had hoped for a boy, and now he had been taken away from me before he could breathe his first breath of life. I was utterly distraught, and Simon was left with arranging for the funeral by himself.

Between our financial loss and the baby's death, psychologically I could not remain in Boro Park. And so we moved to Attorney Street on Manhattan's Lower East Side. The apartment was cheaper and it was also near our new store.

As Simon made his rounds with his hosiery clientele, I had the job of managing the store. Looking to avoid putting all our eggs in one basket in this store, I began contacting various manufacturers in order to find suppliers of other products: children's wear, sweaters, ladies dresses, underwear, etc. In short, Laufer's Department Store, was indeed going to be a department store with an array of different merchandise.

With Lea's continued help (she took care of the children while I minded the store), Simon would be out all day seeing wholesale customers, and I answered the phones and solidified our retail business selling children's dresses and sweaters. We kept the store open from Sunday until Friday afternoon. Simon, from the male chauvinist school of business, initially believed that women didn't know enough about commerce to truly be successful. But soon enough he realized how wrong he was. "I see how the register is ringing when you are present," he would say to me.

And, indeed, with G-d's help, the store did well and we made back the money that had been lost.

At about this time, I opened another store on W. 36th Street and 6th Avenue. Lea, having proven herself a loyal and trusted friend, was placed in charge. In the meantime, a wonderful neighbor by the name of Rose took care of the children and often brought them to our store to see Mommy and Daddy.

But times were changing. By 1957 hosiery sales had declined in favor of the vastly expanding panty-hose business. Yet G-d continued to smile upon us. One day Simon was made an offer he couldn't refuse. One of our clients, a Cuban customer, offered to buy the entire contents of the store — lock, stock, and barrel. A deal was quickly made, at a tidy profit, and the Laufer Department Store became history.

In 1958 Simon opened the business he would run for the rest of his life: L & Z Knitwear, a wholesale sweater distributor. All of his loyal employees went with him to the new location on Orchard Street, except one: me. The time had come for me to take care of the house and our children. And, after all, I was pregnant again.

Simon had an uncanny ability to do business. Though basically uneducated (the Nazis having closed all schools to Jewish children), he was a shrewd visionary. Simon would go to a manufacturer and literally buy his entire inventory of close-outs. It made Simon a popular buyer. It also gave him a price edge in selling his merchandise wholesale. Needless to say, under Simon's astute management, the company grew and eventually moved to larger facilities in Greenpoint, Brooklyn.

By this time the East Side had given way to a home in Hillcrest, Queens, a new and vibrant young Jewish community where Rabbi Sholem Kowalsky was the spiritual leader. Our daughters, who had been attending the Bais Yaakov on the Lower East Side, were now enrolled in the Yeshiva of Central Queens.

Adding to the joy of our move, in 1958 I gave birth to Gayle.

Hillcrest was a beautiful suburban area with grass and trees, far away from the hustle and bustle of the Lower East Side. Here were new neighbors with whom to develop budding friendships and young children for our children to play with. Everything was great — except that there was no real shul to speak of. A small group of people davened at a nearby rundown building, but the facilities were meager and the operating funds nonexistent. Sometimes the members had to daven by candlelight because there was no money to pay the electricity bill.

Though I now had yet another young child to take care of, a dear friend, Zeva Groob, convinced me to get involved in the shul's Sisterhood. "Why me?" I asked.

"Because you are a businesswoman and you'd be able to do it."

"But I'm just a greenhorn," I responded. "What do I know about organizations?"

"We feel and we know that you'll be good," she said. "You have business experience and ability."

I was hooked.

Soon I was very involved with the Sisterhood, essentially a small group run by two or three women. It wasn't long, before I was asked to become its president.

Hillcrest was but a fledgling community in the late 1950s, and it didn't have much in the way of facilities, programs, or anything else. With young children to take care of, the idea of getting involved with the Sisterhood at the executive level was daunting. In addition, since most of the women were Americans and I was essentially an outsider — and a greenhorn to boot — I did not exactly feel comfortable assuming a leadership position. Who would listen to me? What experience did I have with such women?

In the meantime, Simon and I were on our way to Israel to visit his sister Chana. In an act of unexpected graciousness, the community threw us a going-away party and, upon our return, greeted us

Hard at work for the Hillcrest Sisterhood, 1961

very warmly. With the wonderful way they treated Simon and myself, I could no longer say no to the Sisterhood presidency. In 1960, Fran Laufer, a refugee from Chrzanow, Poland, became president of an American Jewish organization, the Sisterhood of the Young Israel of Hillcrest.

Seeing that the shul had no money and that the Sisterhood was financially strapped as well, I organized a board of eighteen women and initiated programs to raise money for the congregation. We would drive to Manhattan to visit wholesalers and factories together with some ladies like Lilli Cohen. At 7 or 8 in the morning I would say to Lilli, "Are you ready?" and we would be off soliciting merchandise for our fundraising activities. We held rummage sales and bazaars, had lunches, card games, sold wine — in short, we did anything possible to raise funds. One lady, Frieda Goldstein, was simply amazing. She was placed in charge of selling fabrics and she made so much money by the way she did things. She was simply wonderful. Rabbi Kowalsky was also very helpful with his guidance and encouragement. It made a lot of us work harder.

Of course, Simon was a major help as well. Through his business contacts and those of other shul members, we were able to get some of the items for our sales events.

It was at this time that I met a young woman who to this day plays an important part in my life. Sara Teicher had just moved into the community. When I met her I recognized a woman of intelligence and an exceptionally good worker. I immediately drafted her and put her on our board. It was a decision I never regretted. Sara has been with me through thick and thin ever after.

Needless to say, Max Weil, the president of the shul during my Sisterhood presidency, was always there for me as well, as

Simon holding Torah presented by the Sisterhood under Fran's leadership to the Hillcrest Young Israel.
The keser Torah was a gift from Simon and Fran.

was Ruth Cohler, who made me a co-chairman of our Israel Bonds drive. Ruth was a leader par excellence, and she raised a great deal of money for Israel Bonds. At her side I learned a great deal.

My term ended on a high note. We managed to pay off the Young Israel's equipment bills, we paid for youth programs, in short, whatever we were able to do to assist the shul, we did. Under my presidency, the Sisterhood even had a Torah written that was brought to the shul with great fanfare, with an orchestra and a huge dinner. That Torah we gave to the shul is still there today, a proud testament to our personal success but also of our devotion to this wonderful community. Later, we donated a Torah crown for our Torah with the names of our parents engraved upon it. (Recently, that *keter Torah* was returned to me. I gave it to my grandson, Rabbi

Jonathan Morgenstern, who now serves as rabbi the Young Israel of Scarsdale.)

During the years of my presidency, the Young Israel's membership rolls continued to increase. Though our community was expanding, it presented a problem — a good problem. The shul was simply too small for the members, and people standing in corners or sitting on the floor was not conducive to proper religious observance.

For years there had been talk of building a new shul, but it had remained just that, talk. Nevertheless, there came a time when those who favored construction managed to override the dominance of those who preferred the status quo, so much so that they moved to elect a new shul president whose main goal would be to foster that construction.

Over the years, Simon's generosity and business acumen had gotten him noticed. He had also long been noticed as a *baal tefillah*, the prayer leader during services.

Simon had a beautiful voice that rose above his fellow daveners when chanting the prayers. When he led the services, his voice reflected the deep feelings pouring forth from his heart. Each time he recited a prayer, his *ehrlichkeit* evinced the feeling that he was in direct communication with G-d. Shul members would especially relish the services when he was the *ba'al tefillah,* and they came to love and respect him. Here was a *mensch* with an easy manner, a pleasant soul, one truly looked upon by G-d with great favor.

As a man of action and accomplishment — at a time when action and accomplishment were most needed — Simon was chosen and then elected president of the Young Israel Synagogue of Hillcrest.

I recall when they came to congratulate Simon they said to me, "You've had *your* glory, now he's the president." Of

With Rabbi Sholem Kowalsky of the Hillcrest Young Israel, 1970

course, I stayed in the background, but I still had my fair share of involvement. I made parties, held receptions, had a sukkah built in our driveway — I did everything I could do to help Simon. I greeted every person moving into the neighborhood, and I tried to get them involved and make them feel good. Since people liked to move in groups, when they heard that Simon Laufer was president of the Hillcrest Young Israel, they moved in, especially from the Holocaust survivor network.

Simon's job was "simple": build a new synagogue! Now, to raise the money for a new building is not the easiest thing to accomplish. One must be an adept fundraiser, negotiator, politician, and, if need be, an arm twister. A gentle man, *shnorrering* money from others was not something Simon relished. But when it came to *Yiddishkeit*, Simon could be a bare-knuckled fighter of the highest caliber. He was forever supporting yeshivahs, shuls, or other Jewish institutions. And so, for his *kehillah*, Simon was a bulldog in his determination to get a new shul built.

During my tenure as Sisterhood president, we raised thousands of dollars through our fundraising programs. Among the many things that money went for, it was decided to place $4,000 in escrow for the day when a shul president would emerge whose goal would be to build a new shul. That man had arrived — and he was my Simon. The money quickly became the downpayment for the architect who was going to design the new shul. But in order to actually build the shul we needed a lot more money. Though I knew Simon could do anything he set his mind to, I didn't think that it was possible for anybody to undertake such a tremendous job.

At the time, the shul owed a great deal of money. There wasn't a penny to spare and a lot of debt. When my husband became president, not only did he bring a business mind to the endeavor but he also brought something else: he brought unity, he brought peace. People started to look at each other and everybody united. Everyone wanted to be involved. Such was his ability to relate to people and to get things done that my Galicianer husband even managed to have two *yekkes* (Germans) as his advisers.

Max Weil, the chairman of the board, Reiner Auman, the building chairman, Simon, and very often Rabbi Kowalsky all engaged people in their attempts to raise money. Rabbi Kowalsky, especially, had tremendous charm and personality. He was able to get a lot of money because he was a people person, a very talented man. In the past he had always helped people in many, many

Establishment of new Hillcrest Synagogue:
(l-r) Rabbi Sholem Kowalsky; Max Weil, chairman of the board; a Queens assemblyman; and Simon Laufer, president of the Young Israel of Hillcrest, 1964

ways, and now they reciprocated. Another indispensable partner in this endeavor was Jack Cohen, the house chairman. In the early years of the shul's development he played a tremendous role as a great friend to the shul and to Simon. In the years that followed, he was always there for everybody and for the benefit of his beloved shul.

And so money began coming in from all different parts of the congregation. But when that source of funds petered out, Simon contacted business associates and friends who lived outside of the area and convinced them to donate. Nobody could say no to him. Some of our friends even moved into the area. And, typically, Simon, when bills had to be paid and no funds were available, gave his own money whenever necessary. In fact, the cornerstone of the building (a $5,000 donation) bears the Laufer name. Only a handful of people knew how much time and money Simon poured into the construction of the shul. But as the proverb says, "You give, you are (*Gist du, bist du*)."

During Simon's term in office, most of the men on the board were well-educated professionals, some with doctorates. But even though Simon was not an educated man, his leadership skills and business acumen gave him great credibility. Simon's way of doing things was to speak little, do a lot. One of the things he accomplished was to convince the board to get the rabbi a beautiful car — an unusual luxury at the time. "This is our rabbi," he told them. Simon came from the old school; he loved *rabbonim*, and not only Rabbi Kowalsky. In addition to the car, Rabbi Kowalsky received a lifetime contract, hitherto unheard of.

Rabbi Kowalsky very much appreciated Simon's efforts and all the effort he was expending on building the new shul.

*At the groundbreaking ceremonies for the new
Hillcrest Young Israel, 1964: (l-r) Alex May, Rabbi
Sholem Kowalsky, Rabbi Hill and Simon Laufer*

With Simon he had a president that other shuls were jealous of. Many presidents came after Simon, but I feel that he was a role model for all those who followed. To build a building, to make a job which is impossible possible, that is a very difficult thing to do.

Of course, the outcome was a foregone conclusion. Though normally the shul presidency was but for a two-year term, Simon was given a third year so that he could finish the building. And finish it he did. By the end of his term, a new shul had been built.

On November 6th, 1964 Simon was honored for his efforts:

> Shimon Laufer,
>
> President of Young Israel of Hillcrest,
>
> is honored this Sunday in a
>
> Charity Federation Breakfast.
>
> *The elite of the Orthodox community of Hillcrest, Long Island and the surrounding areas will honor the well-known Orthodox community leader, Mr. Shimon Laufer, this Sunday, Nov. 8, 10 a.m. at a breakfast for the benefit of the Charity Foundation to be held in the Young Israel of Hillcrest 169-09 Jewel Avenue, Flushing.*
>
> *Mr. Shimon Laufer is president of the Young Israel of Hillcrest and an important supporter of Yeshivahs in Israel and of the local Jewish needy. Under his administration and thanks to his work and aspiration, the Young Israel of Hillcrest built a new synagogue which is a true sanctuary and a powerful center of Torah, prayer, and education for the entire region under the spiritual leadership of the prominent leader, Rabbi Shalom B. Kowalsky.*

At its eighteenth annual dinner, Simon and I were named "Mr. and Mrs. Young Israel of Hillcrest." Friends made during our almost twenty years in Hillcrest turned out en masse.

Hillcrest is the place where our fondest memories were made; it is the place we lived the longest, the place we put down our roots. It is where we established ourselves. Today, the community continues to thrive.

Chapter 7

Family

In September 1947 I found out that I was going to be a mother. For Simon and me, this news was the greatest fulfillment of our lives. I could not believe it was possible for me to bear a child, after the Nazis had forced us to swallow drugs that took away our womanhood.

In truth, we were poor, but we never felt that way. We were satisfied with everything we had. Simon still worked as the cleaning man at Bartons on 34th Street, and he also sold eggs to his co-workers, so the $20 a week became almost $28. I made $24 as a salesperson in Barton's chocolate store on Church Avenue. I travelled by trolley from Powell Street and Sutter Avenue in Brooklyn, to Church Avenue, Flatbush. The stops were sharp and shaky and I often felt nauseous. I worked throughout the nine months of my pregnancy so that when the baby was born, we would have the money to surround the baby not only with love, but with a touch of splendor as well. But I always thanked G-d for bringing me to this wonderful country — America, and for the gift of a new life growing inside me.

My daughter Lottie was born May 8, 1948, weighing 8 lbs. She was a beautiful baby, healthy in every way. Lottie was named after my mother and Simon's mother Lotte Zlate and Mindel. Two days after Lottie was born, while I was still in the hospital, we all received a great gift. The State of Israel was born. Would we have had Israel a few years earlier, perhaps our nearest and dearest would not have been killed.

We took home our crying bundle of joy. Lottie had colic for months, and she spent most of the day crying. Simon and I were thrilled we had a baby. Who could have imagined that we would survive and bring children to the world? Who would have dreamt that we could perpetuate the names of our forefathers, fathers, mothers, sisters, and brothers, and build a bridge into the future?

And G-d had prepared help for us. As we crossed the storming ocean on the *Ernie Pyle*, another miracle happened. We met an angel, a fifty-year-old widow, Esther, going to Pittsburgh. Esther liked us very much, and when we parted, she made me promise to call her when I would have a baby. She would help me and teach me what to do, she told me. When I brought Lottie home, Esther arrived from Pittsburgh. We could not afford a nurse. I had no mother to help me. But G-d was taking care of us, sending us the help we needed.

Now I see the bustle and excitement when my grandchildren and great-grandchildren are born. The new baby is showered with gifts, and the mother is fussed over, treated to healthy, nutritious food, and made to rest. All my neighbors in America had family; as Holocaust survivors we were alone. That was part of our pain, and it never went away. In fact, each time we celebrated joyous life-cycle events — a birth, a baby's first steps, a first day in school, a wedding —

our loss was highlighted anew and our laughter mingled with tears.

After Lottie was born, Simon stopped working as a cleaner. As he told me on that ghastly ship: "I will work for somebody else only to get a chance to get to know my way in America." And so, even though his English was not yet fluent, he struck out on his own. His first business venture was peddling hosiery, and each week was more successful than the last. Some survivor friends were jealous and counted the empty boxes that he threw out to know how much he sold. In time, Simon saved enough to open his own hosiery store.

Nineteen months later, another joyous bundle was born — Suzie, Shulamith Ruchel, named after my Daddy Shlome. It was November 1949, four and a half years after Liberation. By now I was an experienced mommy, and we moved to a big apartment in Brooklyn.

Simon, Fran, and their daughters

In 1951 we moved to Boro Park. Simon was moving up the step ladder, and I was pregnant again. Being new in the area I asked for recommendations for a private doctor — a first for me. The woman who worked in the grocery store recommended the best. But in the fifth month, when I did not feel the baby, all he said was "you're too fat." I said he was no good. But, I had no family, no *bikur cholim* organization to tell me to just find a better doctor.

On *erev* Yom Kippur, as everyone was heading to shul for *Kol Nidrei*, I was rushed to the hospital. I was in my eight-month. We had no-one to leave the children with, so Simon did not come along to the hospital. I was all alone.

The hospital did everything they could, but the baby died. I almost died as well. Simon buried the baby. It took me a long time to get over it — the aborted life of our only baby boy. I had to move from Boro Park not to be reminded of this terrible tragedy. Today I often tell patients, "If you have no confidence in a doctor, find another one. Don't be embarrassed, don't feel bad to change."

In 1951, after we lost all our hard-earned money, we moved to a cheaper apartment on Attorney Street on the Lower East Side. Lottie and Suzie attended Yeshiva schools. They were growing up. When I was working in the business, I made sure that they always had a caring nanny to look after and supervise them. Simon did well in wholesale hosiery. The Lower East Side was not a place where we wanted to bring up the children, so we moved to the suburban community of Hillcrest. When Suzie my youngest was ten years old, I became pregnant with Gayle.

Did the fact that Simon and I were survivors affect our children?

It certainly did. Simon gave in to all the children's whims.

Simon

In turn, they loved him dearly. I, being a realist, was more in control and more authoritative. Indeed, I never enjoyed the same relationship with my daughters as Simon. I find that American children's relationships with their parents are quite different from what we had with our parents. European children were taught and brought up to idolize their parents. My children, and so many others, never had the *zechus* to see how I dealt with my parents — treating them with a reverence that would be reserved for G-d. The girls felt that our home was more serious, and that issues were more black and white; unlike American homes, there were no shades of gray. Our children grew up without knowing or feeling a grandmother's arm, but until they became parents themselves, they did not know what they missed. Although every moment was lived in its shadow, for ten years we never spoke about the Holocaust.

By the time Gayle was born, we were well-off financially, and did not have to worry as we had done. We were able to spoil Gayle in many ways.

In 1965 we led Lottie to the chupah. Three years later, it ended in divorce. Those were difficult years for all of us. Lottie came back to live at home. I was then a serious student in Queens College under the tutelage of Professor Ernest Schwartz. The subject: philosophy. The professor gave me credits for the work I did in the community of Hillcrest. As much as I enjoyed the studies, when Lottie got divorced and came home, I couldn't continue.

Simon and I took Lottie to Israel to give her an injection

of joy and vitality. Simon was a workaholic, but he took time off for his Lottie. We were all over the moon when Lottie remarried in 1971. She had three wonderful children — Dr. Shlomo Morgenstern, a pediatrician, who married Faygie Mendlowitz, and has three wonderful children: Alexander Simon, Chase, and Cordelia. Yocheved Morgenstern married Mark Schwartz, and has four beautiful children: Tyler, Olivia, Madison, and Israel. Rabbi Jonathan Morgenstern married Jordana Wolfsohn, and has four beautiful children: Simon, Ayden, Ella, Yaacov Isaak.

At our oldest granddaughter's wedding

In 1967 we led Suzie to the chupah. Allan Rozner was a wonderful human being and they had a very happy life together. They had four wonderful children: Daniel, who married Suri Sternberg; Cindy married Menachem Pinter, they have four wonderful children, Jessica, Gabrielle, Allan, and Simon.

Lauren married Michael Zuckerman and they have four wonderful children, Reena, Shira, Avi, and Simon. David married Gitty Goldfarb. Allan did not live to participate in his wonderful children's weddings or David's bar mitzvah. At the age of thirty-eight, Allan succumbed to a brain tumor. David was three years old at the time. Suzie, of course, was inconsolable.

As their grandfather, Simon now became a father-figure as well. Years later, Daniel recalled that experience:

"When I was a little boy, I loved spending time with you. I remember when you used to take me, Shloimie, and Yocheved to Great Neck for Shabbos. After spending a wonderful Shabbos together, you would take us for ice cream. I remember those nights at the ice-cream store. We'd sit around and you'd say, 'You lucky stiffs.' Only now do I realize how lucky we truly were.

"When I was eleven years old, our relationship was transformed. When my father passed away, you also became a father-figure to me. Make no mistake, the passion that I felt as a little boy was still there, only now you became a role model and teacher, too. During those years you taught me how to overcome life's most difficult challenges. You also taught me how precious family is, and how family should be cherished by creating a home where Torah values prevailed.

"When I look back at the relationship we developed, it's no surprise that these were our closest days. The time we spent together revolved around your life's greatest passions: family, business, and helping others. We would spend time together almost every day. If you weren't teaching me a new business lesson, then you were teaching me lessons in life. You taught us, cared for us, and supported us in ways that only a father could."

Suzie remarried in 1992. Her husband, Albert Fiderer, was a good husband and a loving father. In 2006, Albert succumbed to lung cancer. Suzie and the family miss him greatly, especially David. Albert was the father David remembers.

In 1977, in the presence of 1000 guests, Baby Gayle married Josh Yashar, a skillful entrepreneur. Their son Jeremy married Jennifer Zombek, and they have an adorable son Jacob. Jaclyn married Brian Glicksman.

During the war, in the midst of the terrible atrocities, I never imagined that I would live to have children who would carry the names of their perished ancestors. G-d has surely blessed us.

All the great-granddaughters

Chapter 8

The Fran Laufer Collection

After his term as president of the Hillcrest Young Israel and my term as president of the Sisterhood, Simon really began to expand his business, manufacturing and importing sweaters. He established a contact in Hong Kong and soon began importing sweaters from there as well. Sometimes, I even accompanied him on his business trips.

China was a wonderful experience for me: all the furnishings and artwork appealed to my creative sensibilities. Enamored of the many beautiful things I saw there, I began thinking of ways to share these things with others and perhaps develop a business of my own in the process. It was then that I made up my mind to get a degree in interior design.

What made me choose interior design? First of all, I had always had a good eye for color and a way with style.

My first preference was, of course, for the world of fashion, but the fashion industry is a weekend-centered affair and, being *shomer Shabbos*, this was out of the question. Interior design, on the other hand, was a Monday through Friday business.

International Society of Interior Designers distinguished service award, 1988

To better learn the field I enrolled in the New York School of Interior Design. I was a quick learner and also had a great deal of life experience to assist me in my studies. At the same time, I attended the Fashion Institute of Technology. Two years later, in January 1974, I became an official interior designer and I had also earned a degree from FIT in fashion design.

I began my professional career doing little odd jobs for friends and family. But on a trip with Simon in 1978, I finally decided to open a showroom of my own, to share with the world all of the fabulous one-of-a-kinds and *objet d'art* I had been finding. The Fran Laufer Collection opened its doors at 200 Lexington Avenue in Manhattan in 1979, stocked with beautiful items I had found on trips to China, Hong Kong,

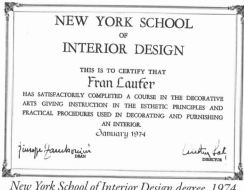

New York School of Interior Design degree, 1974

Bali, Bangkok, Paris, Antwerp, and London.

Number 200 Lexington Avenue had been known for years as a furniture exchange, but not as an interior design showcase. Within two years of opening my 10,000-square-foot place, other decorators began to move in, and soon the building became one of the more popular attractions for interior decorators in the area — and still is.

Thank G-d, the business became very successful. In fact, the International Society of Interior Designers presented me with a distinguished service award in recognition of my dedication to the trade. And Simon, as usual, was instrumental in that success. Every time I went on one of my shopping trips, Simon went with me. Using the tact and psychology that had helped him succeed in his business for so many years, he helped me get the best prices for my acquisitions. One of the things we learned on these trips was to buy items before the New Year. The Chinese believe that if you sell something before then  you will have good luck throughout the coming year. Simon took advantage of that.

And so we bought lots of art and antiques. In every country we visited I secured crates of tapestries, wall hangings, puppets, *objet d'art* — whatever struck my fancy and tastes. Eventually, the Fran Laufer Collection was represented in many decorators' showrooms throughout the U.S.A.

• • •

Traveling to Asia on our shopping trips was usually a wonderful experience — but not always an easy one. In 1980, a year after China opened its doors to visitors, we went on our customary business/pleasure trip to Japan, but this time we decided to visit Shanghai and Beijing as well. As the plane landed in Shanghai, we were told that there would be a bus waiting to take us to our hotel. Unfortunately, our itinerary had been changed and we were not told the name of the new hotel where we would be staying.

As Simon and I disembarked and proceeded to board the waiting bus, Simon suddenly remembered that he had left his scarf on the plane. We both went back to the plane to retrieve it. When we returned a few moments later, we discovered that the bus had gone. I cannot describe the annoyance and anger I felt. At that time, there were no airport facilities — no offices, no stores, nothing. Here we were in this primitive place with no language, no telephone, no door to open. Where should we go? Though I can speak five languages, Chinese is not one of them. All attempts at communication met with blank stares. Even Simon, who I could always look to for the solution of a problem, was at a loss.

An hour passed, with our frustration and bewilderment rising and rising, when suddenly we saw a cab approach. We managed to stop him and tried to communicate with him, asking him to take us to the hotel whose name we didn't know. With our hearts pounding, all of us total befuddled, he dropped us off twenty-five minutes later at a hotel — unfortunately, not ours. As I tried to communicate with the receptionist there — me with my European accent, the desk clerk with her total lack of English. I kept using the word "vegetarian" as a way of describing our group. As luck would have it, a man in the lobby witnessed the scene. Perhaps he was a government functionary, because he spoke a little English and knew of a newly-arrived group that would only eat vegetarian food. Relieving the desk clerk of the confusing situation, he took us to a taxi and directed the driver to the hotel which we had been assigned. What a joy to be reunited with our fellow travelers!

From then on, whenever our group left anywhere, we were always counted.

Over the years, Simon and I visited India, Sri Lanka, Bangkok, Hong Kong, China, Japan, Singapore, Indonesia, and Bali — all exotic locations that provided great sources for beautiful items for the Fran Laufer Collection. In Bali, for instance, we were walking through a marketplace when a large Garuda statue caught my eye. We peeked inside the building adjacent to the statue and discovered an old woman wearing next to nothing. Embarrassed by her nakedness, I nevertheless managed to acquire the statue for $200. Two years later I sold the item for $2,000 to an out-of-town collector who needed it for an exhibit.

Everywhere we went we filled containers with *objets d'art* and had them shipped back to the States. Most of these items were antiques or one-of-a-kind specialty items, wall hangings, screens, and porcelains. In the trade I became known as someone with a good eye and good taste. Of course, I loved it.

It was also at about this time that we moved to Great Neck, Long Island, a beautiful town with beautiful houses. Ours was a ten-room Tudor surrounded by greenery, front and back.

I decorated the house with antiques and *objet d'art* that I had acquired during my many trips around the world. It was a delight to entertain there.

Once settled in, we became members of the Great Neck Synagogue, but when Rabbi Lerner became the rabbi of Young Israel of Great Neck, we joined there as well.

It was while living in Great Neck that we became more involved with Israel Bonds and were selected to host a dinner in our home for Yitzhak Rabin. Of course, the dinner was well attended and we managed to raise a substantial amount of money.

At our Great Neck home, 1980

Simon honored at an Israel Bonds event, 1960s:
(l-r) Rabbi Sholem Kowalsky, Fran, Menachem Begin, Simon and Max Weil

Sukkos was a special time for us at our new home. Simon liked to build a large *sukkah* in our driveway, and we would invite many friends for different meals on this *yom tov*, everything done, of course, with our customary panache.

Over the years while living there, I became involved with charitable organizations like Emunah and Ariel. I went on Israel Bonds missions and Emunah missions to Washington. It was a time of great enjoyment.

When the *Algemeiner Journal* celebrated its twenty-fifth anniversary dinner, I was selected to be the dinner chairman. As such, it was my honor to introduce the guest speaker Elie Wiesel. This was my introduction:

Ladies and gentlemen, tayerer schwesters und brider:

When the Holocaust ended and the survivors were dispersed throughout the world, they were greeted with silence, and thus remained silent. Ten years later, the searing words of a young man were placed on the pages of the book Night. *With those words, tonight's guest speaker...opened a door that allowed survivors to become witnesses and then teachers. His words empowered our own and gave life to a movement that led us to this place in time, a time when we know that the Holocaust will never be forgotten.*

This man is a seeker of truth and a speaker of truth and power... He is a teacher and a guide, and although he says not, he is a leader who leads by example, asking humanity to stand together in the face of evil — whether that evil is racism in America or Bosnia, or the hatred of one Jew for another.

As one who, herself, went through the crucible of the

Holocaust, and as one who has been moved and trans- formed by his life's work, I am honored to have been chosen to introduce a man who needs no intro- duction, eine fun inzereh, one of our

Fran with Elie Wiesel

own, our Nobel laureate who speaks for all of us, who touches all of us, and who has made the world just a little bit better for us all. Ladies and gentlemen, Professor Elie Wiesel.

• • •

In 1983 we decided that the commute from Great Neck to New York City was too much of a daily ordeal and rented a pied-a-terre in Manhattan. Originally, we decided to live there during the week and then go back to Great Neck for the weekends, but it wasn't long before we decided to sell our Great Neck home and look for something permanent in the city.

After extensive searching, we found an apartment at the newly-built Trump Plaza and moved there in 1984. Decorating the apartment was an immense pleasure for me, with acquisitions from the Fran Laufer Collection liberally sprinkled about.

I decorated the apartment primarily in Art Deco and Art Nouveau styles brought from Paris. On a trip there with Simon, I acquired thirty-eight Art Deco chandeliers, as well as many sculptures and accessories that eventually went into my Lexington Avenue showroom. With the rent constantly going up, the chandeliers provided a wonderful source of income.

Soon after moving into Trump Plaza, we joined the Fifth Avenue Synagogue. I got involved with the Synagogue Sisterhood, and so it was easier for me to find friends and feel at home. Simon found it more difficult. I also joined the Women's Club. It was not long before the Women's Club president

Fran in her Trump Plaza apartment, 1990

approached me to decorate the *shul*'s reception area and library. I felt greatly honored. Eventually, I redecorated the sanctuary as well.

Simon, on the other hand, being a Galicianer, was not as comfortable in this new *shul*. His Yiddish accent, so long a

Rabbi Dr. Sol Roth

positive at the Young Israels of Hillcrest and Great Neck, did not ingratiate him to the upper crust New York society that comprised the membership of the synagogue. But a few years later, when Dr. Sol Roth became its rabbi, Simon was able to establish a personal relationship with him. Simon also cultivated a relationship with the synagogue's famous cantor, Josef Malovany. And so,

Simon and Cantor Josef Malovany, 1990

over time, our social status in the *shul* did indeed change. We made many friends and became proud members of the Fifth Avenue Synagogue.

After completing my job of redecorating the shul, I was asked to become president of the Women's Club. Again, I accepted the position. During my two years in office I was also asked to decorate the rabbi's apartment on Madison Avenue.

My two years as president of the Women's Club were very rewarding. The wonderful programs, the shows, the lectures, the parties...all the money we raised for *tzedakah*. Maybe others have had the same experience, but this time was mine, it bore my stamp, and I am proud of my tenure and my accomplishments. Besides the joy of accomplishment, I learned the travails of politics, of rote and archaic practices and procedures, of circumventing roadblocks and recalcitrant people whose dedication to self overwhelmed our true mission of dedication to this synagogue and *Yiddishkeit*.

• • •

The real estate slump of the 1990s brought with it a slump in the interior design business. It was at this point that I decided to close the showroom and devote myself instead to the charitable organizations with which I was involved. Though I had enjoyed the work and found it challenging and exciting, I knew that there would be many things in my life that would provide me with opportunities to keep busy.

Interestingly enough, years later, in October 1996, though I was no longer in the interior design business, I received an invitation to an auction about to take place in Vienna. After being hidden for many years, looted art confiscated by the Nazis during the war had been discovered and was now being auctioned off through Christie's. I couldn't resist and I immediately purchased tickets for Gayle and me.

Many dealers came from throughout Europe to view the articles up for sale, but I was the only person present from the U.S.

As I walked through the exhibition prior to the auction, a very unusual painting caught my eye. The painting, entitled "In the Schtetl," (by Ludwig Knaus, 1829–1910), depicted a family get-together wherein an elderly, bearded grandfather is seated on a chair surrounded by several of his adoring grandchildren. I was so enchanted by the subject matter that I put in a bid. Unfortunately, I was soon outbid. But, as a result of my bid I attracted the attention of a local radio and television station that asked for an interview.

On the third day of the auction, there was some excitement when an Austrian survivor came forward and laid claim to one of the paintings up for sale. After a brief investigation, the painting was determined to rightfully belong to her and was dutifully returned. This was very satisfying to me. So much had been taken from the *she'aris hapleitah* (Holocaust survivors) that it was gratifying to see some semblance of justice.

Upon returning home to my many projects, out of the blue I received a phone call from a London art dealer. "Are you Fran Laufer?" he asked me, I asked how he knew my name and was informed that he was the dealer who had bought the painting in which I had been interested. He told me that he was coming to America and would like to meet with me to discuss the painting so as to get a deeper understanding of the subject matter. I eventually met with him at Christie's. Because of our discussion, he received enough information to make a tidy profit on the subsequent sale of the painting.

Chapter 9

Rivkah Laufer Bikur Cholim

In 1965, a selfless woman who volunteered much of her time to aiding the sick and needy passed away. Rivkah Laufer, the wife of Rabbi Yitzchak Laufer, was a woman who generated kindness and charity and who "loved each neighbor as herself." She fervently believed that the ill and infirm hold a special place in G-d's heart and that just as G-d visited Avraham when he was ill, we must all follow in His ways.*

Together with her friends from the Sosnovitzer Shul headed by the esteemed Rebbetzin Sara England, Rivkah Laufer went to visit and feed the chronically ill at the Hospital of Jewish Chronic Diseases in East Flatbush every Shabbos. It was a *mitzvah*, a good deed, to visit the sick and brighten

---

* The rabbis infer from Genesis (48:30) that G-d's presence is above the head of a sick person, thus indicating the importance of visiting the infirm (*Nedarim* 40b). The *Shulchan Aruch* goes into detailed discussions of *bikur cholim*, further indicating the importance of the mitzvah.

up their day. Thus, Mrs. Laufer tirelessly visited hospitalized and chronically ill members of her community, bringing them food, company, a hand to hold, a shoulder to cry on. In fulfilling the *mitzvah* of *bikur cholim*, visiting the sick, Rivkah Laufer became a role model of selflessness and caring.

When Mrs. Laufer herself came to be a patient at the same hospital, she appreciated firsthand the enormous necessity for *bikur cholim*. Whenever her friends came to visit, she spoke of the need to continue and expand this most important mitzvah.

Unfortunately, a recovery was not to be. As she lay on her deathbed, Rivkah Laufer asked that her work be continued. After her passing, Miriam Lubling, her very close friend, organized a meeting of friends and family at the Sosnovitzer *shul* to create a *bikur cholim* organization that would perpetuate Rivkah Laufer's legacy. A dynamo of a woman, Miriam Lubling, who was later to become Rivkah Laufer Bikur Cholim's National President, spearheaded this effort.

But having an idea does not bring an organization into being. With a $1,000 gift from Rabbi Yitzchak Laufer, Miriam was directed to contact a cousin with business and organizational skills who might help propel the group into successful operation. I was that cousin.

My duties as president of the Hillcrest Sisterhood now behind me, I met with Pearl and Miriam and became involved in what would become a lifelong project. Miriam Lubling, Bella Brodt (later Brodt-Sorotzkin), myself, and Rivkah Laufer's own daughters — Pearl Pinter, Rachel Fischer, Leah Goodman, and Frieda Laufer — would soon build the foundation that has since become one of the most effective and far-reaching *bikur cholim* societies in the world. Pearl, in particular, has continued to involve her entire family in her

Rivkah Laufer Bikur Cholim Luncheon, late 1960s:
(standing, l-r) Pearl Pinter, Linda Mandelbaum, Judy Summers, Regina
Gutfreund, Eda Kaminsky, Frieda Laufer, Helen Lubliner, Jean Gluck, Lola
Tenenbaum, Sara Teicher; (seated, l-r) Miriam Lubling, Regina Peterseil, Fran
and Melanie Berger

service to Rivkah Laufer Bikur Cholim. Together with her husband Mordechai and her children, she is involved in every detail of the organization's operations, particularly at Maimonides Hospital in Brooklyn. So extensive are her efforts that the hospital even offered to pay her a salary. She refused.

In addition to offering advice, companionship, and goodwill, we also had to provide medical and social assistance for those who could not afford it. Doctors and hospitals had to be paid when those who had no money needed medical attention. Facilities had to be provided for the religiously observant who could not travel long distances to visit ill family members. And all of this required money. And so, fundraising became an integral part of our activities.

After our first meeting, held at the home of Bella Diamond in Crown Heights, Brooklyn, friends that I had made at the Young of Israel of Hillcrest came to my assistance. Sara Teicher, Jean Gluck, Regina Peterseil, and Rozanne Rosenthal, were quickly on board — and have been on board ever since.

In addition to the Queens chapter, two other chapters were created as well: one in Crown Heights, which ultimately moved to Flatbush in Brooklyn, and another in Boro Park, Brooklyn. (These successful Brooklyn chapters continue to thrive. In Flatbush, Margo Sledzik, Ruthie Braunstein, Miriam Beer, and Chani Leifer lead a vibrant organization, while in Boro Park, Chani Kofman, Rozi Hellman, Gitty Lichtenstein, and Laya Ziskind invigorate yet further the Bikur Cholim movement. In Manhattan too, Bernice Schwartz, Ann Hiltzig, Ann Ehrlich, and Katho Kahan continue Bikur Cholim activities.)

• • •

Since I had the space in my Queens home, it was decided that our first fundraiser would be held in my back yard. Such was the goodwill toward the project that over one hundred people attended and dined on the home-cooked meal prepared by our wonderful volunteers. Simultaneously, under the stewardship of Bella Brodt, who had been a nurse in Russia after the Second World War, and who would go on to become our national president, another event was held at the home of Gisela and Herbie Freshel in Brooklyn. (Eventually Bella became our contact person for the who's who of medical personnel. Whenever someone needed a specialist, we would turn to Bella. Later she moved to Israel, where she continues to run our *bikur cholim* services.) Rivkah Laufer Bikur Cholim was on its way. A year later, in 1966, I was named the founding president of Rivkah Laufer Bikur Cholim.

Though I was very busy with my business, this organization really struck a chord with me. Through all the earth-shattering events of my life, I never forgot the lessons of *chesed* and *tzedakah* I had learned as a little girl in the Bais Yaakov in

Chrzanow, Poland. After having lost sixty members of my immediate and extended family, surviving slave labor, and having been liberated from Bergen-Belsen, I set out to defy Hitler's Final Solution. This was part of that mission. And not just for me. For the first time, these predominantly European women, many themselves survivors of the Holocaust, became engaged in philanthropy of their own, exclusive of their husbands.

As the organization grew, each year another volunteer stepped forward with her home as the next site for our annual fundraiser. And again, the valiant ladies of Rivkah Laufer Bikur Cholim cooked, prepared, set up, and presented a wonderful affair for all the guests. When the group became too large, we even used the facilities of the Young Israel of Hillcrest. But soon we outgrew even this location.

Eventually, we met the wonderful Lorraine and Sholem Nelson, who were like angels for us. Sholem had a catering hall on Utopia Parkway, and he offered us his facility for our functions. Literally giving us everything we needed at cost, between our volunteers and his efforts we continued to grow and raise the funds needed by those constantly asking for our help.

All the volunteers who give of themselves and their resources to make the organization a success continue to feel the glow of *chesed* that so engulfs all who participate in this noble venture. Instead of being ladies of leisure, enjoying world travel and self-pampering, the women of Rivkah Laufer Bikur Cholim visit hospitals and help those in need. As one patient wrote, "Your joy when a patient feels better seems to come from the bottom of your heart."

The hospitals we visit are very receptive to our efforts. Mount Sinai Medical Center, New York Hospital-Cornell Medical Center, NYU Medical Center, Sloan-Kettering, the Calvary

Working together to help our fellow Jews:
(l-r) Pearl Pinter, Miriam Lubling, and Fran

Hospice, Maimonides Hospital, St. Francis, and Methodist Hospital all make it possible for us to function effectively, and enable us to make a hospital stay more comfortable.

• • •

In the meantime, Miriam Lubling moved back from Israel and told us of the immense need for Israelis to receive medical care in America.

Though today Israel is a modern-day technological wonder, forty years ago it had neither the doctors nor the facilities to take care of its people. For those who needed special treatment not yet available in the young country, their only recourse was to seek medical attention in another country, usually the United States. And, of course, they didn't have the funds to pay for such treatment. We were moved to help. Many patients were thus brought to American hospitals, specialists secured, and their bills paid through our efforts. As Israel has progressed technologically, the need for Israelis to come to America for treatment has decreased, but South American Jewish patients have now made their way to our shores for assistance.

One of my fondest memories involving an Israeli patient and our efforts on her behalf involved a great doctor, Dr. Fred Epstein. A renowned specialist in pediatric neurosurgery, Dr. Epstein was in Israel when we received an urgent plea to help a little girl with scoliosis. Having heard about Rivkah Laufer Bikur Cholim, her mother had called me asking if I knew of a doctor who could treat her daughter. Not only did I know of one, but he was in Israel at the time at a convention. I managed to reach Dr. Epstein and, through Miriam Lubling, arranged for the doctor to see the child. By the time the convention was over, Dr. Epstein had finalized all the details of the surgery.

Within months, the family came to the United States and the patient was successfully treated. In a letter of thanks, the patient's mother referred to our energy and dedication in making the impossible possible. Regrettably, Dr. Epstein was injured in an automobile accident shortly thereafter and subsequently died at an early age. Nevertheless, a miracle had taken place, and a beautiful child was spared a life of pain and disfigurement.

As usual, Simon was always there to help me with his goodwill, his financial support, and the tremendous spirit of *chesed* that surrounded all his endeavors. Unbeknownst to me — and something I wouldn't discover until years later when going through some old paperwork — he had also paid the doctor and hospital bills for some of our patients, albeit without anyone's knowledge.

• • •

Over the years, the scope of RLBC (Rivkah Laufer Bikur Cholim)'s activities and services have expanded. Today, its activities touch both the local community and people needing its help from abroad: medical care is provided for the indigent through subsidies; referrals and appointments are made; patients who are housebound or who cannot make their own way to health care appointments are provided with transportation. In fact, RLBC was the first *bikur cholim* organization to purchase a bus for Rodeph Chesed, an organization that transports wheelchair-bound patients, and it also provides financial support for Kesser Malka, which provides transportation for patients to Manhattan hospitals. RLBC organizes volunteers to visit area hospitals, nursing homes, and shut-ins to make sure patients' needs are met and to distribute Shabbos candles; it has apartments available near major hospitals in New York for use by patients' families on Shabbos and holidays. A state-of-the-art *bikur cholim* room has been created at NYU Hospital, fully stocked with all kinds of amenities and food for everyday and Shabbos needs, and holiday parties are held in hospitals and nursing homes.

In addition to local activities, patients from abroad continue to be helped. In Israel, Rivkah Laufer Bikur Cholim gave financial aid to emergency clinics in Emanuel, Beitar, and Arad; purchased emergency equipment for the 127-year-old Bikur Cholim Hospital in Jerusalem; maintained a Shabbos apartment near Hadassah Hospital; built a convalescent wing in Eiym V'Yeled; donated vital medical equipment for Hatzolah units in Nof Ayalon; supplies a bus in B'nei Brak for volunteers to visit hospitals; built an ambulance shelter in Hashmonaim; purchased a specially equipped bus for Alei Siach, an organization for mentally disabled children and young adults, enabling them to be transported to and from various acitivities and therapy sessions; helped build two playgrounds at the Sulam Institute for Special Children in Jerusalem; provided significant funding to Refuah V'Yeshua, an organization that provides supervised care for special children as a respite for their burdened families; and donated funds to Shema Koleinu, a school for the hearing impaired.

I find the playgrounds at the Sulam Institute especially poignant. Each piece of equipment is covered in padding so as the children rub against them they enjoy the experience of being touched, the experience of being hugged — something missing in their lives.

• • •

For me, Rivkah Laufer Bikur Cholim resonated on a personal level. Dealing with patients became a full-time commitment. No matter the amount of time it required, the work it took to find willing honorees, secure donations, get programs designed and printed, deal with caterers, organizing florists (who provided their services at no cost), arrange for transportation, and all this while dealing with medical institutions and medical personnel for those in need, the feelings engendered outweighed all the effort.

I used to be a regular visitor to Cornell-Presbyterian Hospital. When I walked through the hospital halls, my heart always beat faster as I sought out the rooms of patients I knew. But my heart always skipped a beat when I opened a door and a stranger's puzzled expression greeted me. Nevertheless, I always overcame the awkwardness of the situation.

Years ago, Cornell-Presbyterian was a very cold place for Jewish patients. I would go there three times a week to visit whatever Jewish patients I could find, to add a little *Yiddishe hartz* (Jewish heart) to those who felt alienated during their treatment there. Once, I approached the head doctor and asked him why the hospital was so unfriendly to its Jewish patients. He was stunned by my question and immediately introduced me to the director of patient administration. It had never occurred to him that anyone could have such a perception. As week after week went by I became more and more friendly with that director of patient administration, Susan Mascitelli, who has since done everything in her power to change the atmosphere in the hospital. But I will let Susan recount our relationship.

> Dr. David B. Skinner, a renowned thoracic surgeon from the University of Chicago was recruited to become the president and CEO of New York Hospital (now New York Presbyterian Hospital) in 1987/1988. Dr. Skinner was literally "larger than life," at about 6' 3" and about 230 pounds. He had a huge, deep booming voice and started every day by greeting everyone he saw with a huge: "Good morning!" that shook the roof.

> One day, in 1991, he called upon me to please join him in one of the Board of Trustee meeting rooms where he was seated with several members of the Jewish community from New York who had come to meet him and talk to him about the hospital and the relationship of the hospital with its constituents. When I came into the room, I was not clear what the meeting was about or why he had asked me to join him but it became clear very quickly.

> At that time, I was the Director of Patient Services for New York Hospital, which meant that my staff was the Patient Representatives who helped patients, families, and staff with a myriad of issues. The issues ranged from complaints, concerns, communications, requests, referrals, ethical dilemmas, adverse outcomes or medical errors, and managing very high profile patient needs. Dr.

Skinner introduced me to this large group of people and in his typically loud, authoritative voice, he announced that "This was the person who would be able to help all of you and take care of you and your colleagues' needs and requests!" He encouraged everyone to listen to what I could tell them about the hospital and my staff and then to accept my business card and call upon me when help was needed.

Everyone listened and asked a few polite questions. Then the session was over.

As we were leaving the Board Room, a very sweet, soft-spoken woman approached me and asked if she could talk to me privately, a little bit more directly than possible in the meeting. This woman was Fran Laufer. She was there representing the Rivkah Laufer Bikur Cholim.

Fran and I spoke on that day and we spoke many times and met many times following that day. Fran and I became friends. I could see that with each time she called upon me, her passion for helping others and for finding "the best" doctor for each and every person she advocated for was unwavering and unbending. Ever respectful, she would call and wait for an answer but she would never give up and she would never take no for an answer. Fran always found a way to help. From people in New York, who had the means to pay for the best care but couldn't get an appointment quickly enough, to children and others from Israel and other countries who didn't have a penny in their pocket, Fran always found a way to make it happen.

One day Fran said to me, "You know, I used to come to this hospital and feel like an orphan... When Dr. Skinner introduced me to you, everything changed and we built a bridge together and now I feel like I am welcome and this is my home."

We often spoke about that moment when we realized that we had built a relationship of mutual trust and respect and love for each other that was "meant to happen" so that so many other people could find the help they desperately needed.

In 1994, Bikur Cholim honored me with a beautiful award at Terrace on the Park at their annual luncheon. My family and friends came to meet this special woman and to see and hear about the amazing story of her life and her commitment to this lifelong cause of doing good deeds to help people get the right medical care.

When Fran's beloved husband Simon died, I went to her apartment and visited her. I wondered how she would go on after all of the years of devotion and love that they had. I underestimated my dear friend. Fran Laufer was put on earth to fulfill a mission. She has done this every day of her life. She has suffered pain and tragedy that is unspeakable. She has also enjoyed the beauty of three beautiful daughters and many, many grandchildren and great-grandchildren. Most of all, she has lived her life the way it was meant to be — giving to others and doing for others — in a way that has come back to making her the remarkable woman that she is today. The Rivkah Laufer Bikur Cholim is more active than ever. Fran's daughter, Gayle, is now the one that comes to New York Presbyterian Hospital and makes a difference in the lives of so many patients.

I am now the Vice-President for Patient Services for all of New York Presbyterian Hospital (five campuses) and run an international program for the Hospital. Dr. David B. Skinner died several years ago but is remembered every day. The bridge that he helped Fran and I build is stronger than ever and will only grow stronger and wider because of Fran's mission and legacy.

• • •

These days, Rivkah Laufer Bikur Cholim associates are fully recognized by the hospital staff and are counted on to aid patients. Among the many things we do there, is supply Shabbos candles, prayer books, and even stock refrigerators with kosher food. Like me, my daughter Gayle Yashar and Esther Weinberger also make Cornell-Presbyterian the venue for their *bikur cholim* duties, and Zelda Berger visits St. Frances Hospital.

In addition to Cornell-Presbyterian, I often visited other New York-area hospitals as well. Each place has memories of people met, of friendships made and of friends thus made and lost.

Over the years, Miriam Lubling, Pearl Pinter, and I have witnessed many miracles, one of which still moves me to this day. On one of my visits to Sloan-Kettering Hospital, I met Faygie, a beautiful 17-year-old girl, the victim of a rapidly spreading cancer. Beside needing a high-risk bone marrow transplant, her chemotherapy and assorted other treatments were extremely painful, leaving her weak and dispirited. Terribly depressed by her condition, each day she crept closer to the entrance of the World to Come.

After meeting her, it wasn't long before there developed a bond between us. Whenever I came to the hospital I would immediately seek her out, and she began to look forward to my visits as well. Then came the High Holy Days and Sukkos. While I was away, her treatments continued. Though she battled the cancer that was eating away at her, her strength diminished each day. Her family, continually at her bedside, became more and more distraught.

When I finally managed to get back to Sloan-Kettering, I brought her a little gift. She was very happy to see me. When I looked at her and realized how emaciated she had become, it broke my heart. And then I held her hand, took a deep breath and told her about the Rivkah Laufer Bikur Cholim Luncheon we have each year in June. I told her that I wanted her to be my guest of honor. I don't know what possessed me, but I told her that I wanted her to be there and that she must look deep inside her soul and determine that she wanted to live.

Miracle of miracles, she soon went into remission. On June 10, 2004, my newfound friend walked to the podium at our luncheon at Terrace on the Park and delivered a heartfelt speech to the men and women assembled. There wasn't a dry eye in the place. Thunderous applause greeted her words.

Not long after, she met a wonderful young man who had survived his own battle with cancer. Today, they have a four-year-old son, named Immanuel, meaning "G-d is with us."

But not every story has a happy ending. I also met a wonderful young woman, a mother of ten, who had come to America from Israel for treatment. Although her family stayed by her bedside day and night, she finally succumbed, despite chemotherapy and a bone marrow transplant. Though

I barely knew the woman, her death was devastating to me. Some time later, upon the upcoming marriage of her daughter, her husband sent me a very touching invitation.

Dear Mrs. Laufer:

One of my wife's outstanding characteristics was gratitude and its expression. During her illness, she kept a log of those who did her a good turn or even smiled at her. "When I get well," she explained, "I want to express my gratitude to each and very one."

Consequently, I feel obliged and privileged to express our appreciation for your kindness during this most difficult period of our lives. As one is suspended between heaven and earth, any hand extended with goodwill is embraced warmly. The solace offered is etched in our hearts in perpetuity.

We hope as you shared in our times of sorrow, you'll share also in our time of simchah.

Of course, I attended this very meaningful wedding.

Another person I met who has had a profound affect on the Rivkah Laufer community is Suri Spierer. Fifteen years ago she lost her daughter, Chane Rivky, to hepetoblastoma, a liver tumor. While she cared for her daughter for three months at Memorial Sloan-Kettering, I would often visit. Suri insists my visits brightened her day. Suri was so appreciative that after her daughter passed away, she decided to do something in her memory. And so, she started a food program that delivers home-cooked meals to hospitals all over New York, Boro Park, and Flatbush. Today, she is in constant demand from our three bikur cholim organizations. With the help of a volunteer organization she has developed, she services thirty to forty families a night and fifty families on Shabbos and *yamim tovim*. It is amazing how such wonderful happenings can come forth from tragedy.

• • •

During all the years of my hospital visits I helped so many people and, I hope, in some small way, I affected their lives for the better. But it wasn't until years later, when Simon became ill, that I discovered an additional mission for Rivkah Laufer Bikur Cholim.

The development of managed health care means that the medical system no longer operates the way it used to. Although there are still excellent physicians who handle their patients with care and sensitivity, the system of medicine has become callous and unfeeling. Today there are gatekeepers who determine whether you can see a doctor or receive a special test; there are nurses who determine whether you can be admitted to a hospital and whether your insurance company will pay the bill. In short, medicine has become a business, and while insurance administrators concern themselves with profits, lives are at stake.

Our new job at Bikur Cholim was to become advisers to patients and relatives, to make them informed consumers. They had to learn how to be assertive with a doctor, how to get information when little is forthcoming, about the need for second opinions, and of the necessity to be on top of things to make sure that a loved one is getting the proper care. In my husband's case, had it not been for my questioning the drugs being administered, there would have been fatal consequences. These days, lack of information can lead to a life-and-death situation.

The mitzvah of *bikur cholim* is one of the most important acts of humanity a Jew can offer another human being.

Extending a hand during the heat of illness, affording companionship when one is afraid and alone, helping when one is in need, these are what make *bikur cholim* so meaningful and demanding. Yet not everyone has the grit to witness the pain of a child, to see the tears and terror of the terminally ill. The men and women of *bikur cholim* are a special breed of people whose hearts and minds, entwined with a devout belief in G-d and Torah, accept the challenges, conquer them, and keep coming back for more. I am grateful for the small part I am privileged to play in this special mitzvah.

Chapter 10

Return to Roots

In 1985 Simon decided that he wanted to return to Krakow, the city of his birth. I was hesitant — after all, the Communists were still ruling Poland and I felt it might be dangerous. Eventually I agreed to his going, but under one condition: that he bring back a *sefer Torah* that had survived the *Shoah*. I felt that this would provide a sense of divine purpose to his trip and that G-d would thus help him to return safely.

Once in Krakow, Simon located the building in which he had lived and knocked on the apartment door he remembered as a child. When the tenant inside answered the door, Simon explained who he was and asked if it would be possible to just view the home in which he had grown up. Surprisingly, he was shown in. For Simon it was a pleasurable but emotional experience. It reminded him of when he was a child sitting with his father. Later, he told me how he remembered everything about Krakow, so much so that he was even able to direct taxi drivers — because they weren't as familiar with the city as he was.

The Remu Synagogue entrance

Sure enough, Simon returned with a *sefer Torah* from the Remu Synagogue of Krakow. The Remu, Rabbi Mojzesz (Moses) ben Israel Isserles, 1530–1572, was a renowned rabbinic sage of the Middle Ages. Known as the Polish Maimonides, the Remu was also a *rosh yeshivah* and an astronomer, a mathematician, a philosopher, and a historian. His most famous work is the *HaMapa*, a commentary on the *Shulchan Aruch*. Because of his reputation, his synagogue has remained a regular pilgrimage site for thousands of Jews during the Jewish holidays, especially on Lag B'Omer.

There is an apocryphal story concerning this famous shul. In Europe it was popular to celebrate weddings on Fridays. The Friday night meal thus became the wedding feast and the first of the *sheva brachos* — a cheaper option for all concerned. And so, in a house near the courtyard of the shul, a wedding took place on a Friday. The celebration was joyous and musicians played. Rabbi Isserles, coming to the shul for *Minchah*, heard the music wafting into the shul, and he asked the band to stop playing, as Shabbos was rapidly approaching. Though the celebrants were thus warned, the musicians played on — even as the *Ma'ariv* was well underway. Suddenly, the

The Remu Synagogue courtyard with commemorative plaques on its wall

house collapsed and all inside perished. From then on, no Jewish weddings in Krakow took place on a Friday.

The synagogue's interior features include the original *aron hakodesh* (built some time after 1557) as well as the steps, pulpit, and *ner tamid*, all of which were added after the war. The foundation plaque has remained, as well as another one, next to the *aron hakodesh*, commemorating the place where the Remu used to sit.

The Remu Synagogue survived World War II without any damage. However, when the Germans turned it into a military storehouse, it lost its interior features. The *bimah* from 1958 is an exact reconstruction of the one from before 1939. Both the southern door (from around 1670) and the northern door (from the second half of the 18th century) are original.

Outside the shul is the Old Cemetery (dating back to the 16th century), the most ancient in Krakow. Over the years it fell into disrepair, and many of the headstones were destroyed. No more than a dozen of the graves with headstones including that of the Remu are actually burial sites. It is said that during the war the Nazis sought to destroy this gravesite as well. The first workman to touch the headstone fell over dead, and the project was abandoned. The cemetery received some repairs in the 1950s with many headstones placed in orderly rows (regardless if or whose body was under them). Fragments of headstones were also collected and built into a "wailing wall," recalling the Kotel. Today, the cemetery is more of a museum than a functioning cemetery.

Having survived the war, the shul was still in use but it had hit upon hard times. Since most of the Jewish Polish population had been killed or driven away, it was difficult even getting a minyan for daily services. Simon convinced the *gabbai* (caretaker) to sell him a *sefer Torah* to take to America for use

The first of its kind placed in the courtyard of the Remu Synagogue, Simon ordered this plaque to memorialize our families lost in the Holocaust. (Unfortunately, they misspelled my name.)

by an appreciative *kehillah*. While there, Simon also had a special plaque commissioned and installed in the shul courtyard commemorating our parents.

Communist Poland forbade the export of any Jewish books or printed materials, and Simon had to plan carefully to be able to bring the *sefer Torah* back home. Simon brought with him an old siddur and on his entry papers, declared possession of a Jewish holy book. When it came time to depart, he once again declared in his possession a Jewish holy book. To the ignorant Polish customs agents, a Jewish holy book is a Jewish holy book. Thus Simon was able to bring a *sefer Torah*, the greatest of all holy books, out of Poland.

This special *sefer Torah* was brought to America and examined by a *sofer* in Monsey, New York. For the next twenty years, the *sefer Torah* was zealously guarded until the moment for its donation to the right organization. In the meantime, whatever needed to be done to insure the Torah's integrity was done.

In 2006, the Torah was brought to Israel and presented to the Israeli Defense Forces' 97th regiment, the *Nachal Chareidi*.

In 1989, Simon made a second trip to Europe, but this

Simon standing in the Fuchsbrumer apartment in Chrzanow. His grandfather's apartment is to his left. Tante Surcie Apfelbaum's former store is directly below (the one with the Produkcji Rolnej sign).

time the whole family went along. We went to Chrzanow, Auschwitz, and Bergen-Belsen. We showed them everything.

I had hoped to visit the gravesites of my paternal grandparents, who had died before the war, but their headstones had been removed and so we weren't able to locate their graves. As for visiting the graves of my immediate family — my parents, Lotte Fuchsbrumer (née Goldberg) and Shlomie ben Ichack, my brother, Ichack ben Shlomie, and my sister, Golde — as well as aunts, uncles, and cousins, were all murdered in Auschwitz. For them there is no gravesite, no place at which to say Kaddish, no headstone on which to leave a pebble. Their gravesite is only the dust and ash of that accursed concentration camp.

Simon at the Auschwitz exhibit, 1989

Chapter 11

Anniversary Waltz

On March 17, 1991, we celebrated our "second" wedding in Tavern on the Green. For hours, a resplendent cotillion of guests and friends celebrated with us. I was radiant in my long, ivory wedding gown especially made for this occasion. My groom, Simon, beamed with delight. He was dressed in a tuxedo and a bow-tie, and he didn't stop murmuring "Such a surprise, so unexpected, this is something I would never have imagined..."

What we were really celebrating was our forty-fifth anniversary and Simon's seventieth birthday. Without Simon knowing, we sent invitations to several hundred friends, and we prepared a video that we showed at the reception. For weeks I worked late into the night to prepare all the details, while everyone made a real effort to make sure Simon didn't find out what was going on under his nose. But Simon knew something was cooking — maybe because I had asked him to prepare a speech to give at the fictitious birthday party of a friend. Even if he did guess, I don't think he grasped the mag-

An anniversary celebration to remember

nitude of what we had actually planned.

The main ballroom of Tavern on the Green was tastefully decorated, the musicians played romantic melodies, a wedding canopy was in place and we were married again, just like a young bride and groom. I noticed people in the hall wiping away a tear or two.

Rabbi Sholem Kowalsky, the former rabbi of the Young Israel of Hillcrest, returned to America especially to celebrate with us and be the *mesader kiddushin*. He explained to the crowd why and how after forty-five years we were making a second wedding. He assured everyone that Jewish law would not be broken — there would be no specific marriage blessings made. Further, the glass would be broken (to remember the destruction of the Holy Temple) by me, the bride, instead of by Simon, the groom.

And then it was time for the festivities to begin. Our guests watched wide-eyed as the bridal procession marched down the aisle.

The rabbi of Young Israel of Hillcrest, Rabbi Simche Kraus, Rabbi Arthur Schneier, the rabbi of Park East Synagogue in Manhattan, Rabbi Sol Roth of the Fifth Avenue Synagogue, and Rabbi Marc Schneirer of the Hampton Synagogue, all spoke about the different meanings of happiness. Then Cantor

Joseph Malovany sang the blessing on the wine, and Rabbi Kowalsky took a sip. The cantor sang "If I Forget Thee, O Jerusalem," and Rabbi Schneier said a few words and warmly wished us good fortune and happiness.

I broke the glass and the musicians played wedding melodies and our friends and guests could not stop saying, "Such a tasteful party, what a pleasure."

The *crème de la crème* of Orthodox Jewish society was there, among them real-estate developer George Klein and his mother, Regina, members of Stephen Klein's family, the man who had brought us to America. George told Gershon Jacobson, the *Algemeiner Journal* publisher, that a couple who had been through so much deserved the joy of celebrating a second wedding.

It was a party that was "both sacred and humane," as Toby and her husband said, "without a doubt, without any hesitation, one of the most beautiful parties we have ever attended."

Simon thanked Cantor Malovany for his beautiful singing with a kiss. William Mandel, the treasurer of the Kielce Society and Marvin and Eli Zborowski, founder of the American Society for Yad Vashem, and Sam Skura noted: "Let the enemies of Israel see how Holocaust survivors celebrate their existence. It's a holiday of the victory of 'handing over many into the hands of the few.' "

R. Moshe Braunfeld, a well-known leader of Holocaust survivors, a longtime friend of Simon's and a businessman from Boro Park, said that our party was truly one of the miracles of our generation. Moshe Mruwka, a Jew from Chestochowa, who spent the war disguised as a German soldier, said: "Who could have imagined in 1945 that in 1991 we would celebrate this way in New York in the Tavern on the Green?" Rabbi Shlomo Trau agreed.

The enthusiasm of our guests was genuinely felt in the air, and seen during the spirited dances. The guests danced with the groom and raised and lowered him on his chair exactly as is done at a regular Jewish wedding.

Our grandchildren recited poetry with a traditional rhyming melody in our honor. Every one in the crowd received two pages of verse, so all could follow along as they sang the story of our lives. They sang about our charity and good deeds, our support for Bobov and R' Meir Baal Ha-ness in Jerusalem, our work for Rivkah Laufer Bikur Cholim.

Our daughters and sons-in-law were no less radiant than we.

Abraham Obstfeld, who was together with Simon in Auschwitz, was also at the party, and he confided to Cantor Malovany: "Who would then have believed that we would be privileged to celebrate in such an amazing fashion?"

The evening ended with a sentimental speech by Simon.

> Life is like a dream, he began. On March 21st I will be seventy years old. What I went through in life normally one hundred people do not experience... In 1942, they took away my parents, my brothers, and my sisters to the Krakow Ghetto. I never saw them again. I had already been arrested by the SS and was in prison, chained together with other Jews awaiting deportation to Auschwitz... Today, forty-eight years later, my clever family surprises me with the most beautiful birthday any man could ever dream. Yes, life is a beautiful dream. And why not? Looking around I am surrounded by my dearest children, my grandchildren, and my very dear friends. No, I did not forget my dearest *kallah*, Fran, last but not least. To you my dearest Frimciu, I like to say that you are

the apple of my eye. My love for you gets stronger every day and every year. *Shlomo HaMelech* had one thousand wives, but none of them was as good as you.

Simon then went on to thank our children and grandchildren for the honor and recognition they showed him. He closed his speech with a heartfelt thanks to our guests.

Then I made my own speech, describing the forty-five years we had spent together. All the promises Simon made when we were engaged — that he would be my husband, but also my father, mother, brother, sister and care-giver — thank G-d, he kept. I was truly fortunate to be his wife.

We raised our three daughters to be Torah-loving and observant Jews, and our grandchildren and great-grandchildren follow the deepest traditions, staying true to their Torah roots. Our family has triumphed over Hitler in the very way he feared the most. He wanted to destroy us in order to destroy the Torah, but we make it live and breathe. As the scholar Cassirer said, "The victims of this ordeal cannot be forgotten; the wounds inflicted upon us are incurable. Yet amidst all these horrors and miseries there is, at least, one relief. We may be firmly convinced that all these sacrifices have not been made in vain.

Just like the Jews of Sinai, we, the Jews of Europe, went through the *kolos u'verakim*, the thunder and the clouds of smoke, the lightning and the terror of the sound.

The Jews of Sinai came out of that darkness into the freedom and the light of the Torah. Maybe because I risked my life on the death march to help a friend, Hashem wanted me to survive — perhaps to help others and to teach my children to follow in the path of His ways as described in this parashah. I, too, came through the *kolos u'verakim* to say "*Na'aseh Ve'nishma.*"

This week, so near the anniversary of the liquidation of Chrzanow, we are reminded by this parashah of why we are Jews, of what we said and how we said "*Na'aseh ve'nishma* — we will do and we will listen.*" When we appreciate the full extent of this commitment, we carry out our mandate as a holy nation and continue to experience that unique revelation, the Torah, Hashem's way, that has guided our people from the past through the present and will guide the generations ahead.

Chapter 12

Simon's Legacy

Having been a student at the Bobover Yeshivah in Poland, Simon was an ardent supporter of the Bobover Rebbe, Rabbi Shlomo Halberstam. Simon would always recount that during the war, "thanks to the Rebbe's influence I was strengthened in my faith in conducting the struggle against the Nazis... The Rebbe's words gave me the strength and the vigor to bear the trials, pain, troubles, and persecution of the murderers."

Once in the United States, Simon remained close to the Rebbe and his Rebbetzin and frequently participated in events honoring them. In addition, Simon donated to Bobover institutions, including a *beis medresh* in Boro Park.

Simon's dedication to the Bobov dynasty was again reinforced in a special reception for the Bobover Rebbe. Opening the doors to our Upper East Side home, Simon welcomed the Rebbe, his *gabbai*, Rabbi Shmuel Horowitz, Yehoshua Shternhel, and a

Fran (right), with the Bobover Rebbetzin and the Rebbetzin's daughter, Rebbetzin Chumi Tauber

few dozen Bobov chassidim. Said Simon: "For me it's an outstanding privilege to be able to greet the Bobover Rebbe and his chassidim. When I languished in Bochnia more than fifty years ago, I could not have imagined that I would greet the Bobover Rebbe in my house. Now I am thankful to G-d that He bestowed upon me this rare privilege."

Present at the reception were local area rabbis and community leaders, businessmen, politicians, and other prominent people with whom Simon had made connections over the years. As he walked around the room, hugging and kissing friends and acquaintances, his tear-filled eyes expressed the depth of his emotion. "Blessed are You our Lord, who let us live and kept us alive and brought us to this time," he exclaimed.

Bobov wasn't the only chassidic institution which was the subject of Simon's largesse. He was one of the primary supporters of the Trzebiner Yeshivah in Jerusalem and other religious organizations. Over the years, Simon and I were honored by literally dozens of Torah observant organizations, from Mesivta Tiferes Yerushalayim to the Trzebiner Yeshivah, from Yeshivas Chasam Sofer to Orthodox girls' schools. In fact, Rabbi Kowalsky once noted, "One could write whole books about the good deeds of Shimon and Fran Laufer."

Such was Simon's dedication to Jewish learning and Orthodox observance that in 1994 we were honored by Ariel, the Israeli institution. Elie Wiesel was the guest speaker.

Simon and the Bobover Rebbe, 1990

In his speech Simon recounted, "By G-d's mercy I was saved from inhuman torture and I emerged from the war whole. I saw clear miracles every step of the way, and for this I want to thank Almighty G-d by supporting such institutions as Ariel, Bobov, Trzebiner, and other institutions of Torah and charity."

During that interview I added, "We want to show that despite all we lived through, despite all the trials and difficulties, we, the Holocaust survivors, have to serve as living proof that the Eternal One of Israel

Rabbi Moshe Feinstein with Simon, 1979, in a thank you letter to Simon for his support of Mesivta Tiferes Yerushalayim

does not lie. We must not despair, and we did not, when, after the Holocaust, after having lost everything and everyone, we rebuilt a new Jewish life, established families, stood on our own feet and built up institutions and establishments to extend the golden chain of our parents and grandparents."

• • •

At an AMIT dinner in 1995, I was given the honor of delivering a speech about my husband. With hundreds of people listening I said:

> It's been fifty years since a dashing young man found me among the corpses of Bergen-Belsen. A shadow of the girl I once was, he nevertheless decided that I should be his wife. I had no family — all had been taken away, one by one — and he promised to be my father and mother, my sister and brother, everything I could want. I resisted because I felt I had nothing to give, nothing to offer: my body was a wreck, my tears had all been cried out, my joy in life had been torn from me for what I assumed would be forever. But he persisted, seeing in me more than I could see in myself. And he kept his promise to me. Behind every good man is a good woman. Simon says I have been that woman. But for me, in all my endeavors, there has been a very good man. To my Simon, thank you for being so persistent and thank you for everything you have done to make ours a wonderful life.
>
> Without my Simon, I don't know how I would have found the courage and fortitude to go on with my life. Simon believes the greatest mitzvah is one that is done silently, piously, without fanfare, without expectations

of *kuved*, without expectations of reward. That has been Simon's style throughout his life and throughout our lives together. There are many who can testify to his wisdom, his tenacity, his willingness to help those in need. His success in life reflects his leadership, vision, kindness, and generosity.

In the fifty years Simon and I have been together, we have shared in the birth of three beautiful children and in the birth of our even more beautiful grandchildren. We are grateful for this gift of life, for the ability to bring to this world new generations who carry the names of the loved ones torn from our lives. And we have also witnessed a major victory over Hitler and his Final Solution, the miracle of the State of Israel. *Am Yisrael Chai.*

We, the survivors, can only hope that we are leaving a legacy of courage, determination, and heroism. For fifty years we did everything in our power to convey the message. We built museums and monuments; we inscribed the names of the martyrs on walls of synagogues and Holocaust centers; we published Yizkor books. We traveled to the countries where the carnage took place: concentration camps, cities, and *shtetlach.*

Did it satisfy our own longings for our loved ones, who will never find a resting place? I wonder. They are living forever in our memories and in our hearts. Sadly, with our passing, their faces and images will finally also pass away.

To Rabbi Roth, Bill Schwartz and Cantor Malovany, I wish to thank you for all your efforts and participation in this marvelous function. And to all of you who are here today to share with us this special chapter in our lives, I offer heartfelt thanks. All of you have a special meaning to us."

In 1998, at the age of 77, Simon became very ill. We were in Israel, enjoying Sukkos when Simon had to be rushed to Hadassah Hospital by ambulance. Then came the news: Simon had colon cancer. We quickly returned to the States, where the diagnosis and prognosis were confirmed.

Although he was in great pain, Simon, as usual, suffered quietly, not wanting to upset the family. But whether at Cornell, Lenox, or Mt. Sinai hospitals, a family member was always at his side. In the meantime, as there was no treatment that would provide him any relief, I went online and found natural remedies that promised some help. After obtaining them, I forced Simon to swallow the herbal concoctions and, miracle of miracles, they caused the symptoms of his colon cancer to subside.

Confined to his bed, Simon would sing *nigunim* and re-member the days of his youth, his family, and his life before the war. As our hopes rose that he would have some relief from his illness, a new diagnosis indicated that he now had leukemia.

On the fourth day of Av, 5758, Simon Laufer, the man who had promised to be my father and mother, brother and sister, the king who made me his queen, passed away. Written on his gravestone, inscribed in Hebrew, it states:

Here lies buried a man raised above the average, beloved and easy-going, a loving and dedicated husband and fa-ther, a beloved grandfather, Reb Shimon Zelig, son of Reb. Sholem Laufer of Krakow. A firebrand saved from the fire

The picture on the right is the horizontal section of Simon's gravestone, with the names of family members who perished in the Holocaust.

Simon's headstone at Wellwood Cemetery, 1999

of the years of anger and destruction, he was exalted by being an admirable link in the chain of the generations. He was the first and the head of all things that dealt with the sacred. His aim was to strengthen Torah institutions and centers of chassidus. He offered charity and help to others in stealth. His essence was good deeds and simple faith and trust in the Almighty. He prayed before others, and into his prayer he poured heartfelt song and petition. He left behind him generations of honest people who follow his path. He was interred with a good name on Monday the 4th day of Av 5758 (1998). He was 77 years old. May his soul be bound up in the bond of life.

The funeral was held at the Wellwood Cemetery in Brooklyn; hundreds of people attended. Many rabbis who had come to love Simon, honored him with extremely moving speeches, as did all of our grandsons.

Our grandson, Jeremy Yashar, was especially poignant

when he remarked:

> Zaydeh was a man of many deeds and few words. His
> deeds were always from the heart and touched the heart
> of those around him. Many of [his recipients] did not
> even know him....
>
> I simply cannot express in a few short moments
> what I have learned form Zaydeh over the nineteen years
> of my life, but I do know that because of Zaydeh I am
> a better person. He showed us that the impossible was
> possible. With his passing we see how true those words
> really are.
>
> Zaydeh, the special song we sang to you always was
> "You Are My Sunshine." I promise you here today that
> as sure that the sun will rise each and every day, you will
> be in our thoughts and that we will always feel your rays
> of warmth upon us as we continue to make you proud
> and give honor to your name.

Simon's death was so very heartbreaking. We had hoped
that he would live to attend Jonathan's wedding, but it
was not to be. As I sat *shiva* with my children in my home
in Trump Plaza, hundreds of people came to pay their
respects. Friends, rabbis, many of his doctors, there was
always someone calling, someone telling us of Simon's
greatness, of his giving, of his caring and of his love for so
many people.

It was very difficult for me to cope with the pain. Simon
— the strong, powerful, smart, and loving Simon — was gone
from my life. Along with the loss were the responsibilities
that were suddenly thrust upon my shoulders. How does one
learn overnight to handle various business situations? As for

the children, they now had Simon's business to care for on their own. Their number one problem solver was gone; they would now have to fend for themselves.

As a fifteen year old in Chrzanow, each day I had to learn to survive. Overnight, in my later years, I had to learn once again to be independent.

Chapter 13

Deerfield Beach

After having spent a few winters in Miami Beach, where snowbird friends often lived until after Pesach, I decided to buy a place of my own to escape the chill of New York. Looking around, I came upon Deerfield Beach. Sight unseen, I bought a condo because the facilities offered a gym, adult education classes, and a Young Israel that thrived out of a storefront *shul*.

The Young Israel of Deerfield Beach had started in 1980 with twenty people who rented a small storefront for the purpose of conducting religious services. By 2000, the community had grown to require four storefronts. The time had come to consider a building to house the ever-expanding community.

With a donation from the Levy family, the developers of all the Century Villages in South Florida, a 1.73 acre of land was deeded to the Young Israel upon which construction could commence.

Having long had an affinity for Young Israels, and in memory of Simon, I donated to the temple's construction.

Young Israel of Deerfield Beach "The Fran & Simon Laufer Building"

The new edifice would be named "The Fran and Simon Laufer Building."

On February 9, 2003, formal ground-breaking ceremonies took place. On September 15, 2004, the Young Israel of Deerfield Beach, located at 202 Century Boulevard, opened for Rosh HaShanah services.

The main sanctuary, comprising 23,000 square feet, can seat 1,200 congregants and features stained-glass windows depicting the Ten Commandments and the Twelve Tribes of Israel surrounding a custom-designed ark. There are two social/lecture halls, used for the synagogue's study groups, a library, a Sisterhood room, administrative offices, and a chapel for the daily *minyanim*. An acoustical engineer was retained to ensure that any speaker or cantor to be heard throughout the sanctuary. The facility was also made user-friendly for the disabled.

During Chanukah, a special event was held at my home honoring the synagogue's opening. With many guests in attendance at that luncheon, my daughter Gayle stood and delivered the following speech.

> On behalf of my mother, Fran Laufer, and my father, Simon Laufer, *alav hashalom,* I would like to welcome you to the *chanukat habayit,* the dedication of the Young Israel of Deerfield Beach.
>
> It is with a great sense of pride and admiration for my parents, that I can boast of a "*makom Torah* in every port," as my parents have been a driving force in building and establishing shuls and yeshivot around the world. This shul in Deerfield Beach enjoys good company with the Young Israel of Hillcrest in Queens, Shaar Shimon D'Bobov in Brooklyn, the Great Synagogue in Jerusalem, the Remu's shul in Krakow, and certainly Rivkah Laufer Bikur Cholim to name just a few.
>
> The halachah is that a shul and a *beis medrash* do not require a mezuzah on the door post. This is because the reason for a mezuzah is to remind the entrant to be conscious of Hashem always. A shul or a yeshivah do not require this reminder as its very purpose — to be a house of study and worship of Hashem — render reminders unnecessary. I would like to draw the same comparison to the shuls and yeshivot that bear my parents'

The Aron Kodesh of the Young Israel of Deerfield Beach Synagogue, flanked by the specially designed stained glass windows depicting the twelve tribes of Israel

name. When we see the names of Fran and Simon Laufer upon these *mekomei Torah*, we are reminded of their journey, and certainly without the *hashgachah* of Hashem it would not have been possible. My parents survived to live their lives making a *kiddush Hashem*. Indeed they survived, and dedicated their lives to rebuild what they and *klal Yisrael* had lost.

Chapter 14

The Remu
Torah Presentation

The special *sefer Torah* that Simon managed to acquire in the 1980s from the Remu *shul* finally found a new home in Eretz Yisrael, when it was placed in the care of the Israeli Defense Forces' 97th Regiment (the *Nachal Chareidi*, a religiously observant unit) in October 2006.

At a special ceremony that included dancing through the streets, shofar blowing, and the participation of hundreds of people, the *sefer Torah* was carried to its new home at IDF Central Command Headquarters (Metzu-

Grandson David Rozner carrying the Remu Torah during the dedication ceremonies

dat Nechemia) in Jerusalem. Amid great fanfare, the Torah was placed in an *Aron Kodesh* made all the more beautiful by its presence.

Surrounded by Suzie and her family — children and grandchildren — I was honored with a special presentation. As I expressed my thanks to all present, the emotions of the moment welled within me. My voiced cracked during my speech. All that I had experienced during the war and after the war, embodied by the *sefer Torah* that had endured and

The Sefer Torah in the Aron Kodesh at IDF Central Command Headquarters (Metzudat Nechemia) in Jerusalem

survived the same war, overwhelmed me. To have survived where so many had perished and to be standing in a Jewish land in the embrace of a nation of Jews, was an awe inspiring moment for me. My dear Simon would have so enjoyed this fulfillment of his mission to Krakow.

In addition, at the festivities, I was so moved by the spirit of the occasion and by the wonderful young soldiers who so ably defend our homeland that, when I found out about the loss of one of their fellow members, I decided to donate a library in his honor as well. A Torah library to the Netzach Yehuda Regiment, in memory of Sgt. Ro'l Farjoun, who fell in the line of duty in Lebanon, was dedicated on October 19, 2006.

Chapter 15

A Return to Chrzanow

In August 2007, through the efforts of some charitable individuals (Baruch David Halberstam, Samuel and Roman Mandelbaum, and Srulek and Rachciu Wiener) and under the auspices of the Chrzanow Young Men's Association, a *landsmanschaft*, the town of Chrzanow announced to the world a rededication of its Jewish cemetery. Long forgotten, overgrown with weeds and brambles, with boulders and branches contributing to hazardous footing for any who ventured to enter, the cemetery had been cleaned and restored, its broken headstones replaced, and secure walls and gates erected.

The call went out to the former Jewish residents, "Come back."

As the flags of Poland, Israel, and the United States waved in the warm air, Mayor Ryszard Kosowski greeted the survivors who returned to the town that had ostracized them so many decades earlier, a town complicit in the extermination of so many, a town now looking for forgiveness.

Chrzanow, 1980
(Today the town's buildings have been refurbished and the numbers of the buildings changed — effectively obfuscating Jewish real estate claims.)

All this aroused mixed emotions for me. Everything that had been my life in Chrzanow — family, friends, my home, our business — had been taken away. There was no restitution, nor could there be any. Even in the face of the Chrzanower attempts to put a nice face on their efforts, to prevent these very Jews now assembled from ever making a claim on all that that was stolen from them, the buildings in the town had had their addresses changed, further obfuscating the possibility of any claims. Though the mayor may have been attempting to reach out to us, asking for forgiveness was asking the impossible.

Nevertheless, I came, and I brought six of my grandchildren along with me on this journey of remembrance — Cindy and Menachem Pinter, Daniel and David Rozner, Jaclyn and

Brian Glicksman.

In our two-week journey, we went to Hanover, Bergen-Belsen, Prague, Krakow, Auschwitz, Wieliczka, Chrzanow, Majdanek, Warsaw, St. Moritz, Corvatsch, Lovigno and then home through Italy and Switzerland, the beauty of these two countries mitigating somewhat the history of Poland and Germany.

Was the trip worthwhile? Did I really need to come back and once again be overwhelmed by all that happened to me here? I'll let my grandchildren answer for me.

• • •

Dear Grandma,

It is difficult to express in words the emotions and gratitude we feel after a two-week journey that truly was an experience of a lifetime.

We know how difficult it was for you to pick up and go both physically and emotionally at this time, yet you selflessly pushed yourself as you always do to accomplish this goal so you wouldn't disappoint us.

We know how much time and effort you put into planning that each minute would be perfect, and we really appreciate that.

You took us on a journey through time and history that was unique, special, and important for all of us. The importance of what you showed us and taught us by bringing us back to your roots has created a most important link of your past to the future generations of our family.

We can never fully feel the pain you and Zeydeh suffered for so many years or bring back all you lost, but the lasting impressions and beautiful memories you created for us on this most special journey are what words and stories could never fully describe until we saw what we did through your eyes. We have always admired and been so proud of what you and Zeydeh built and accomplished, and now we are truly in awe.

We thank you from the bottom of our hearts for taking us on this life-altering mission and creating bonds and memories to last a lifetime. We will always cherish this wonderful time we spent together.

With much love and gratitude,
Cindy and Menachem

A Retrospective
by Jaclyn Yashar Glicksman

I am a third-generation Holocaust survivor. My mother's parents were victims of the worst crime against humanity. My grandparents are heroes because not only did they survive this darkest period of history, they lived to tell about it and to do what they could to make sure it never happens again.

I always felt special and proud of my heritage because of my grandparents. The names "Simon and Fran Laufer" are prominent in all Jewish places and causes. My grandparents' acts of chesed and endowments of greatly needed funds for various Jewish charities are renowned throughout the world. Whenever I visit Israel, I walk through the front doors of the Great Synagogue in Jerusalem with my head held high, as my grandparents' name captions the entrance way. There are so many other places: Shaar Shimon in the Bobov shul in Boro Park (named in honor of my Zeydeh, Shimon Laufer); the Young Israel of Deerfield Beach in Florida; the Young Israel of Hillcrest; the renowned Remu shul in Krakow, to name just a few. The Rivkah Laufer Bikur Cholim, co-founded and administrated by my grandmother in memory of her cousin, Rivkah Laufer, sets the standard for Bikur Cholim organizations throughout the world. My grandmother is a celebrated guest speaker on the Holocaust.

At Auschwitz exhibit viewing a cattle car similar to the one I had experienced

Recently, my mother and I accompanied my grandmother who was invited by Yale University to participate in their Holocaust Survivor's Archive. All of these involvements and endowments truly testify that Fran and Simon Laufer did not let the Holocaust beat them. They survived, built a family, maintained Jewish practices, and ensured that their precious Jewish legacy would survive as well.

While my grandmother is so committed to ensuring that the Holocaust is never forgotten on a community level, she is even more committed on a personal level. My brother, cousins and I were raised hearing stories of my grandmother's childhood, her sainted parents, and village life. We were always told stories of how she and Zeydeh lived through great challenges. We were enchanted by the story of how they met at the Displaced Persons camp after the war and that my Zeydeh fell in love with a sickly, underweight, malnourished young girl to whom he proposed marriage and vowed to always take care of. We knew first-hand that Zeydeh kept his promise from that day forward and for the rest of his life; my grandmother had her shining knight in armor always taking care of her and making sure that she never suffered another day in her life.

My grandparents took their children, Suzie Rozner Fiderer, Lottie Morgenstern and my parents, Josh and Gayle Yashar, to visit their hometowns and to give them a taste of the *alter heim*. Certainly they all came home enlightened and enriched

Celle shul

by the experience. My mom fondly recalls my Zeydeh energetically running through the streets of Krakow, remembering

Bergen-Belsen monument

places and reminiscing about childhood memories. My grandparents felt that it was important for their children to have this perspective of their family's heritage. Sadly, my Zeydeh passed away in 1998, but my Grandma is determined to continue this charge to keep the children connected to their roots.

This past summer, my grandmother facilitated a life- changing experience for my cousins, my husband and me. My grandmother graciously invited us and escorted us back to Eastern Europe. We visited her hometown, Chrzanow, my Zeydeh's hometown of Krakow, and various other places that were part of our family's heritage. How fortunate were we! While I had already experienced the March of the Living, a school trip to Eastern Europe, and was emotionally charged by that trip, here I would be given the ultimate tour, a first-hand account with the best tour guide possible. While I was excited to be going to the places which played such an important part in my family's history, I was also scared to be in countries that still experience such rampant anti-Semitism. I was also so impressed with my grandmother's courage to go back and face the nightmares of her youth. I didn't have much to worry about. Not only did she face her nightmares, but her feisty personality and boundless energy propelled us through the streets where she held her head up high, and with her regal presence she slew the demons of her youth.

Our journey began in Celle, Germany, a small town, provincial and charming. Its Bavarian architecture gives it a uniquely European flavor, but what made it so special to us, is that it houses the shul in which my Zeydeh and Grandma were married. This was truly a fitting place for us to start our journey, at the very place where it all began. The *aron kodesh* and *bimah* were in good condition, though unfortunately I don't think there are enough Jews in Celle to make regular use of it. We then strolled through Celle searching for the apartment building they first lived in. My Grandma remembered it clearly; not much had changed. Later we went to Bergen-Belsen from where my Grandma was liberated by British troops and we saw the Displaced Persons camp where she survived miraculously before meeting Zeydeh.

Our next stop was Prague, and after Celle, it was quite surprising and satisfying to see that Jewish life still exists there. I wondered why we were here. Again, my grandmother's wisdom became apparent. Prague presented us with a taste of European Jewish life, the way my grandparents had lived before the Shoah. The architectural details and soaring cathedral ceilings all illuminated the rich heritage and tradition that was all but lost to us. We were amused and delighted to see that the ladders which enabled the Golem to escape remain, a remnant of the Middle Ages, and we were comforted to see that memorials to European Jewry are apparent with the names of Czech victims inscribed on shul walls.

Our tour continued to Zeydeh's hometown of Krakow, Poland. We went to the famous pharmacy of Tadeuz Pankiewicz, who secretly opened a wall in his shop which backed the Jewish ghetto. Through this wall he smuggled food, medicine, and information to people in the ghetto. His pharmacy has been commemorated as a museum in Krakow. Imagine our delight to see Zeydeh's name listed as number 249, along with his address and date of birth. Upon seeing his name in print we truly felt Zeydeh with us on our heritage journey.

Our next stop of the day was the renowned Remu shul, the most important Jewish site in all of Krakow. Once again, Zeydeh joined us as we viewed his and Grandma's philanthropic contribution to the perpetuation of Jewish life in his hometown. The plaque that is prominently displayed in the courtyard will bear witness to Fran and Simon Laufer's memorial for all future generations.

After the Remu shul, we went on to Oskar Schindler's factory. Our cousin, Monyek Goldberg, was one of Schindler's Jews, so the factory played a significant part in our trip. When we entered Schindler's office, my grandmother started to tell us stories and, before we knew it, we were surrounded by other tourists, fascinated and privileged to hear my grandmother's eyewitness account. They thanked her profusely and told her sincerely that what she had shared was a highlight of their trip and greatly enhanced their understanding.

Our next stop in Krakow was Plaszów, where my grandmother took us to the grave of Sara Schenirer, founder of the Bais Yaakov movement. As a student of Bais Yaakov, and to underscore her appreciation of her own Jewish education, my grandmother took this opportunity to pay tribute to this valiant woman who opened the doors for Jewish women to have a Jewish education.

Our final stop in Krakow was Zeydeh's apartment building. Once again, we felt Zeydeh with us as we viewed his second-floor apartment from the plaza square. Grandma took us to the square and looked brazenly at each of the residents who were peering at us from their windows. She told us that whenever Jewish tourists come here the Poles are afraid that they will come and reclaim Jewish property. Imagine — the Jews who were beaten and thrown out of their homes by the Poles now impose these feelings of guilt and fear onto their oppressors. Grandma was not intimidated by them; she proudly pointed out familiar places of interest to us, and then we left.

Our trek continued on to Auschwitz-Birkenau. No amount of education or information could prepare us for the horrors that we viewed there, and what made it so much worse for us was the knowledge that our Zeydeh had been imprisoned there. My Zeydeh was a strong, remarkable, loving man, and to imagine that he had to sustain this was overwhelming. My Zeydeh never told me about this horrible time in his life, probably because he wanted to protect me so that I should only know about beautiful things. I thought about this as we saw the crematoria that the Germans tried to destroy when the Allies came to defeat them. They tried to erase the evidence of their evil. I internalized the importance of these Jewish heritage trips to keep the truth alive. Although my Zeydeh tried to protect us, I truly thanked and appreciated my Grandma's commitment to ensuring that future generations never forget.

After visiting Zeydeh's hometown, we went on to Chrzanow, Grandma's hometown. This was truly a highlight of our trip, as the town was rededicating the Jewish cemetery which dates back to the 16th century. Many government officials, members of the Chrzanow Society and their families were there for the ceremony. Grandma was a celebrated guest at this occasion. She joined her *landsmen* and was accorded much honor and respect. She was bombarded by Polish radio and television broadcasters to share her personal reflections of the day. All of her grandchildren proudly stood by as she eloquently answered the interviewers' questions in flawless Polish and were mesmerized by our intelligent and fascinating Grandma.

After the ceremony, Grandma took us on a tour of Chrzanow and focused on the places of her childhood. We visited the site of her family's business, a shoe store, which like everything else Grandma says is "unrecognizable." She explained to us in Krakow that this was done to insure that Jews don't return to reclaim their properties. We saw her family's apartment, situated over the store located in the square, the main thoroughfare of the town, and walked around the building and the courtyard. Grandma took us to a nearby building where she showed us the decrepit stairs to the cellar where she hid during the war. She told us that while she was hiding in the cellar, a kind woman gave her a coat and two silk scarves as she did not think that she herself would survive the war. She instructed my grandmother to give the coat to the woman's son if she ever met him. My grandmother remembered this woman's kindness all these years later, recounting that the coat kept her warm and the scarves were traded for sandwiches for her to eat.

Our journey took us throughout Eastern Europe and we were constantly fascinated by the descriptions and insights that Grandma offered. There is no way that we could ever express in words how grateful we are to our Grandma for making this opportunity possible. We are determined to take this charge that our Grandma has given us and keep her legacy alive. Our Grandma and Zeydeh are true heroes and we are proud to be part of this remarkable family.

On a personal note, I would like to thank you, Grandma, for giving me the opportunity to participate in your book. It is truly a privilege to be your granddaughter and I promise to tell my children and grandchildren your amazing stories and to carry on yours and Zeydeh's great legacy.

Epilogue

I would like, for at least a moment, to turn back the cal-
   endar,
To turn back the pages to yesteryear.
To the town of my young years,
To my school,
My playmates,
To my home,
To the liveliness of the Jewish street.
To Shabbos and the *yom tov* Kiddush and a father's
   honor.
To my father, to my mother, to my sister and brother,
To everything that was in my house and in my life.

The memories remain incomplete.
Even the faces of my dearest and nearest have become
   clouded.
Their ashes were scattered in the death camps,
And in our hearts remains eternal pain.

I cherish memories of a beautiful childhood, surrounded with love from my parents. My mother Lotte was respected and looked up to, not only by the family, but by all that knew her. She had that special wisdom, a modern outlook on life, that few women or men possessed. She was intelligent, wise, dedicated to caring for our every need. In those days, my dear father, Tateshi, had a beautiful black beard. The gray was not there yet.

I learned a lot of *chesed* from my parents. On Friday night or Shabbos lunch, Tateshi often used to bring home poor, hungry men he met in shul. Every Tuesday and Thursday, we had a yeshivah student eat a meal in our house, and of course my friends' parents did the same. The Bais Yaakov education I received in the afternoon did the rest. Charity and *chesed* was a central part of my upbringing.

When the war broke out, our whole world collapsed. Tateshi was forty-nine years old, as was my mother, when the Nazis took them away from me, my brother Benek, and my sister Goldzia (Golda).

My dearest family, my dear friends, almost all were gone. What will happen to me? I asked myself. No home, no food, nobody to lean on. I had to grow up by myself.

Thinking back I wonder, How was I able to go on? The camps, the death march, the death train, Bergen-Belsen, hunger, dressed in rags, typhus... How did I survive? I ask myself. We thought each day might be our last.

What kept me going? I wanted to live. I was hoping to find my parents, my brother and sister Benek and Golda, my aunt and uncles, my cousins. And, I sang. Whenever I had a chance we sang Jewish songs, Polish songs, Russian songs.

There was one message that I kept constantly in my mind:

G-d is looking over me and He will not let me die. I had no siddur, but I talked to Him always, in all places, at all times.

And there were the miracles: While forced to do slave labor in the concentration camp Neusalz, I had a daily opportunity to help myself to a few vitamins that belonged to the SS women who were controlling us. That, surely, was a miracle that helped me survive. There was the time I escaped from the Death March, and found help in a nearby village: another miracle. And there was the miracle of meeting Simon and marrying him — in Bergen-Belsen, in the midst of the ashes, no less.

Two months after Liberation, as I slowly recovered from typhus and was able to stand on my feet again, I started looking around — maybe I could find somebody who once belonged to me, my family. I found no-one. But Simon found me, as terrible as I looked, skin and bones. He fell in love with a skeleton. He was handsome, good looking. I was sick. I felt sorry for him. A good man should marry me?

"Find somebody else, I have nothing to offer," I told him.

"You are everything I want," he said.

I really was not serious or ready for marriage. Simon brought me back to health, and when we married, life began to bloom again.

Being the first married couple in Bergen-Belsen, we matched up many couples and were *interferers* at their wedding — leading then down the aisle. At our own wedding, we were led to the chupah by two widowers. Since we were living in Celle, a town near Bergen-Belsen, we hosted many refugees who kept coming looking for their families.

Coming to America was such an eye opener: we couldn't believe that such a great country exists. Even though Simon and I had to work very hard, we were very happy, only praying to G-d that we would have children. G-d listened to our prayers and gave us three wonderful daughters. All our grandchildren are happily married. We have twenty beautiful great-grandchildren, and one more expected around my birthday on Pesach. Simon would have been very happy. The two of us were never able to hope or dream that we would be able to rebuild a future, and especially and specifically based one Torah, *avodah*, and *gemilus chassadim*.

The scars are there, the pain persists — the grief over lost lives. But so does the pride — the pride of survival. As to the experience itself, looking back today, everything seems to so unreal. Did it really happen? How did we manage to survive, how did we manage to fight back, to resist? How strong our defiance, our will to survive! Quite often it is hard to believe, even for us who were there, that whatever we went through really happened.

But there is not a Shabbos or a holiday where I do not cry at candle-lighting time. I close my eyes and see my parents and siblings, my aunts and uncles and all of the others that I loved and still love who are lost to me forever. When I walk in the street, I still search for them, for their familiar faces... or turn when I hear a voice that sounds like one of them. It never goes away.

At night, I dream. I dream of my life before the war, of the time before they took my parents and family away. And I also dream of what came after. I dream of the people I worked with — forever gone, of the corpses that I saw in piles in the death camps and on the death marches. I cry in my sleep and dream I am once again being beaten or my head is being shaved.

These are not things that one can ever forget...or forgive.

Glossary

Aktion (G) — round up

Alav hashalom (H) — may he rest in peace

Appell (G) — roll call

Aron Kodesh (H) — holy ark

Bekeshe (Y) — long jacket worn by Chassidic men

Bimah (H) — raised platform in the middle of a synagogue
on which the Torah is read.

Chanukat habayit (H) — dedication of a new building

Chassid (H) — hassidic Jew

Cholent (Y) — meaty stew traditionally eaten on the Sabbath

Commandant (G) — commander

Dreidl (Y) — spinning top played on Chanukah

Durchgangslager (G) — transit camp

Einsatzgruppen (G) — police arm of the Nazis

Eruv (H) — boundary around an area (such as a town) allowing carrying outside on the Sabbath.

Gabbai (H) — sexton

Gelt (Y) — money

Goldene medinah (Y) — (literally: golden land), i.e., America

Halachah (H) — Jewish law

Hashgachah — guidance

Juden (Y) — Jews

Juden altester (G) — senior Jew in charge of work camp, affiliated with Nazis

Judenrein (G) — purged of Jews

Kapo (G) — Jewish overseer working for the Nazis

Kehillah (H) — Jewish community

Kiddush Hashem (H) — sanctification of G-d's Name

Kotel (H) — Wailing wall

Makom Torah — Torah center

Mamishe (P) — Mother

Mishloach manos (H) — gifts of food given on Purim

Ner tamid (H) — Eternal light

Niggunim (Y) — melodies

Payos (H) — sidelocks

Raus (G) — Out!

Rebbe (Y) — Hassidic spiritual leader

Sefer Torah (H) — Torah scroll

She'aris Hapleitah (H) — Holocaust survivors

Shnell (G) — quickly

Shtiebl, shtieblach (Y) — small synagogue

Shtreimel (Y) — fur-covered hat worn by hassidim

Shoah (H) — Holocaust

Sonderpass (G) — working papers allowing the owner to work in an Aryanized business

Tashlich (H) — ritual performed on Rosh HaShanah by a source of water.

Tayerer schwesters und brieder (Y) — dear sisters and brothers

Troyhandler (G) — Nazi overseer

Wassertreger (Y) — water drawer

Yomim tovim (G) — Jewish holidays